ALBERT NOBBS

ALBERT NOBBS

by Gordon Steel

JOSEF WEINBERGER PLAYS

LONDON

ALBERT NOBBS
First published in 2003
by Josef Weinberger Ltd
12-14 Mortimer Street, London, W1T 3JJ

ISBN 0 85676 264 4

AMATEUR PRODUCTIONS
Royalties are due at least one calendar month prior to the first performance. A royalty quotation will be issued upon receipt of the following details:

Name of Licensee
Play Title
Place of Performance
Dates and Number of Performances
Audience Capacity
Ticket Prices

PROFESSIONAL PRODUCTIONS
All enquiries regarding professional rights should be addressed to Alan Brodie Representation Ltd, 211 Piccadilly, London W1J 9HF.

OVERSEAS PRODUCTIONS
Applications for productions overseas should be addressed to our local authorised agents. Further details are listed in our catalogue of plays, published every two years, or available from Josef Weinberger Plays at the address above.

SPECIAL NOTE ON SONGS AND RECORDINGS
For performances of copyrighted songs, arrangements or recordings mentioned in this play the permission of the copyright owner(s) must be obtained, or songs, arrangements or recordings in the public domain may be substituted.

Printed by Wrightson's, 2 & 3 Mallard Close, Earls Barton, Northants NN6 0JF.

For our mam

ALBERT NOBBS was first performed by Hull Truck Theatre Company (John Godber, Artistic Director) at the Spring Street Theatre, Hull on April 3rd, 2003, with the following cast:

ALBERT NOBBS	Graham Bill
CONNIE NOBBS	Pamela Merrick
ROSE/ALICE BLUNT	Ruth Carr

Directed by Gordon Steel

Set and Lighting design by Graham Kirk

AUTHOR'S NOTE

The dynamic and exciting unpredictability of the relationship
between Albert and Connie is reflected in the swift changes of
action from scene to scene and from the past to the present.
Rather than have huge, elaborate set changes it is important to
use the audience's imagination to alter location so that the
action of the play flows seamlessly.

The set used in the first production for Hull Truck in 2003 was
a section of a simple multi-purpose living room. To give the
room a universal feel and to reflect the warmth of the relationship between Albert and Connie, the entire room and its furni-
ture was covered in shades and tones of soft orange.

As a symbolic link between the two worlds in Act Two, Connie
appeared in pools of light outside the room to deliver her
monologues. She was used as a link – a narrator – through
whom we were allowed to witness the story.

The Set

The room itself was an island with the carpet and the two walls
being softly and steeply tapered at the edges. A small table
with two chairs was situated up left. Upstage of the table was a
CD player and a magazine rack. To the right of the CD player
was an entrance, which led to the kitchen and outside. Albert's
armchair was situated up right. Upstage of the armchair, right
of centre, was a wall unit that housed the drinks, the crystal
ball, the telephone, a table lamp and a photograph of Mandy.
At the start of the play the unit was pulled down and the back
of it doubled up as the bed. At the end of the first scene Albert
lifted the bed up to reveal the unit. To the right of the unit was
a return that was used as the front hall and contained the coat
hooks. Up centre, left of the unit, was a shelf that contained
CDs and a table lamp matching the one on the unit. Between
the door to the kitchen and the shelf with the CDs was a
concealed wardrobe that was revealed in Act Two. The cupboard housing Albert's football boots was just through the
door into the kitchen and went into the side of the wardrobe.
An imaginary mirror was situated downstage right of centre
and a window downstage left of centre.

Gordon Steel
July 2003

ACT ONE

Scene One

'The Story of My Life', by Michael Holliday plays. A corpse lays in bed. A man grieves close by. The music fades down.

ALBERT   You understood how much you meant to me, didn't ya'? Tell me you understood. I need to know that! 'Cos you did. By bloody hell you did. You were everything to me, Connie. Oh God!

(The corpse sits up.)

CONNIE   I'm dead.

(She goes to lay back down and then immediately sits back up.)

It's not bloody funny.

(She lays back down.)

ALBERT   I know I didn't tell you I loved you very often.

(She raises her head.)

CONNIE   You didn't tell me at all.

ALBERT   But I did, I loved you more than anybody. *(With added gravity.)* I loved you more than Frank Sinatra.

(Music fades out. She raises her head.)

CONNIE   Bloody hell!

(She lays back down.)

ALBERT   Look, I need to tell you something. I know I shouldn't have . . . but well . . . I punched Rose. I'm not proud of it. Well not exactly punched, more physically ejected her from the house. She was poking her bloody nose in. Why can't people just leave us alone? I know this is more than just a little setback, you know, you being dead an' that, but we'll overcome it won't we? Judith's coming to the funeral, but she wasn't very happy, I mean you didn't give her much notice, dying suddenly like that. She's not bringing Mandy, she's got school and she doesn't want to upset her, ya' know, seeing a dead nana.

(*With a sudden burst of anger.*)

What the hell did you do it for? You knew I wanted to go first but no, you had to do it, didn't ya'? Bloody blood clot. Ya spiteful bugger. I bet your bloody laughing now aren't ya'? Well go on then, have a bloody good laugh 'cos I'll tell you this for nowt, it's . . . not . . . funny.

(*He walks round the bed and climbs in next to her. He kisses her and lays down.*)

Goodnight, Connie.

CONNIE   Goodnight, Albert.

(*He starts whistling, 'There May Be Trouble Ahead', from Lets Face the Music and Dance.* CONNIE *sits up.*)

He always whistles when he's nervous.

(CONNIE *gets out of bed and moves down left into a pool of light. Music in under dialogue, 'Lets Face the Music and Dance'.*)

We always said, goodnight, every night before we went to sleep, and then we'd kiss. We never missed. And there I was, cold and stiff as a board and he slept with me like he'd always done. We'd been married for thirty-five years.

(ALBERT *gets out of bed, tidies it away and exits.*)

Fought like cat and dog. Never had a good word to say to each other – that's love. It's 'cos he's bloody awkward. He does things just to be awkward. He enjoys it. He's not happy unless he's miserable. Things started to take a turn for the worse the day Albert retired from work. He was terrible with food but I'd actually managed to get him on to pasta and I couldn't believe it the next morning when he actually agreed to go to the shops and get some mince.

Scene Two

Lights up in the room. ALBERT *enters, wearing a coat and cap.*

CONNIE   You managed to find it, did you?

ALBERT   Funny.

CONNIE   Didn't get lost.

ALBERT   Here.

(*He throws a white plastic bag at* CONNIE, *which she catches. She looks in the bag.*)

CONNIE   What's this?

ALBERT   A packet of mints.

(CONNIE *pauses, looks out to the audience disgusted and then pulls a packet of mints out of the bag. She turns to* ALBERT.)

CONNIE   For the lasagne.

ALBERT   You said a packet of mints.

CONNIE   Not, Mint bloody Imperials, you stupid bugger. You've done this on purpose.

ALBERT   Go yourself next time.

CONNIE   If this is what retirement's gonna be about you can go back to work.

ALBERT   It's me first day off.

CONNIE   And it'll be your last if you carry on like this. (*To the audience.*) This is what he's like, contrary as the bloody weather.

ALBERT   (*pause, then ruminatively*) Hey, it doesn't seem like forty years. Forty years.

CONNIE   Where's it all gone?

ALBERT   Sod knows. Forty bloody years.

CONNIE   It's a long time.

ALBERT   It's a life time.

           (*Pause.*)

ALBERT/   Forty bloody years.
CONNIE

ALICE   (*off*) Coooeee.

           (ALICE *enters.* ALICE *wears a shiny, yet worn, shell suit. She hasn't got her teeth in.*)

ALBERT   Oh God, here she is, laughing gas.

CONNIE   (*aside*) Alice lived over the road, bless her.

ALICE   (*blunt*) I couldn't sleep. I can't sleep these days. Never slept for weeks.

ALBERT   Morning, Alice.

ALICE   Is it? Why is it? 'Cos it bloody isn't.

CONNIE   What's bothering you, Alice?

ALICE   I've lost me teeth. Couldn't sleep for thinking about it.

CONNIE   You'll've just mislaid them.

ALICE   I've looked everywhere. (ALICE *farts.*) Ooh, that's better.

ALBERT   Bloody hell, Alice!

CONNIE   Alice!

ALICE   Eeh, I'm sorry, but I can't keep owt down these days. They want me to go in hospital to have one of them things up me . . . you know . . . they want me to have a cafeteria.

ALBERT   (*humours her*) Bloody hell, Alice, I think you've got a dead ferret up there.

ALICE   It's those pickled onions I had. I love 'em you know, but they don't like me.

CONNIE   Would you like me to come and look for them for you?

ALICE   The pickled onions?

CONNIE   Your teeth.

ALICE   I can't find 'em. I've looked everywhere.

ALBERT   It hasn't spoilt your good looks though, Alice.

ALICE   (*coyly*) Stop it.

ALBERT   You're looking as gorgeous as ever.

ALICE   He's such a flatterer.

CONNIE   Isn't he just?

ALICE   How you handling retirement, Albert?

ALBERT   A lot better since you came in.

ALICE   I was a tacker down Smith's Dock.

CONNIE   (*aside*) She never failed to mention work.

            (CONNIE *exits*.)

ALBERT   Did you used to have some laughs?

ALICE   Eeeh, we used to have some laughs.

ALBERT   Was it ran by a small family firm?

ALICE   It was ran by a small family firm.

ALBERT   I bet you miss it, do you?

ALICE   By hell I miss it. You never get over it, you know.
          It's like having an arm off.

ALBERT   Well, that's nice to know.

ALICE   You'll end up talking to yourself. It comes to us
          all. One minute you're as right as rain and the next
          your as mad as a wasp.

ALBERT   Well, that's cheered me up.

ALICE   And then there's the loneliness.

ALBERT   Sommat to look forward to, then.

          (CONNIE *enters, wearing a cardigan and carrying
          a plant which she places at the centre of the
          table, left*.)

ALICE   When I get down, I find the best cure is to laugh.

CONNIE   Well then, I think Albert's gonna struggle.

ALICE   You just pop round to our house, I'll show you a
          good laugh.

ALBERT   I couldn't trust meself in a house on me own with
          you.

ALICE   (*coyly*) Shurrrup. He's a bugger. (*Chunters as she
          exits*.) Where the hell have I put me teeth! If that
          bloody dog's had 'em again I'll swing for 'im.

ALBERT   If I ever end up like that, bloody shoot me.

CONNIE   And me.

ALBERT   She's as mad as a fish.

CONNIE   We haven't done so bad though, have we?

ALBERT   You're lucky you've got me.

          (*She looks at him in disgust.*)

CONNIE	Phugh! You begged me to marry you, you did.
ALBERT	I was trapped.
CONNIE	Begged me.
ALBERT	I can remember it as plain as day. We'd just come out of the pictures.
CONNIE	That's right.
ALBERT	We'd been to the Odeon.
CONNIE	We'd been to The Lyric.
ALBERT	The bloody Lyric – on Bolckow Road.
CONNIE	It's not there now.
ALBERT	It was a Saturday night.
CONNIE	It was a matinee.
ALBERT	And you dragged me into that bloody show house.

(*They don't move apart from simultaneously snapping their heads – they are now in the show house.*)

CONNIE	It's a bit small.
ALBERT	It's bloody tiny. You couldn't swing a cat round in here.
CONNIE	That's disgusting.
ALBERT	What?
CONNIE	Swinging a cat round.
ALBERT	It's just what people say.
CONNIE	Which people?
ALBERT	Any bloody people.

CONNIE	There's no need to swear. It'd be nice though, wouldn't it, if it was ours?
ALBERT	What?
CONNIE	I can't stand flowers on the wallpaper.
ALBERT	Whoah. Whoah. Look, I know I'm a good catch.
CONNIE	Fancy yourself a bit, don't ya?
ALBERT	Understandable though, isn't it? I like me own space. I can't see me settling down for a long time yet.
CONNIE	Well that's alright, 'cos I'm gonna get married.
ALBERT	You'll make someone very happy.
CONNIE	But I don't wanna marry someone like you.
ALBERT	Well that's alright, then.
CONNIE	I wouldn't entertain someone like you.
ALBERT	Good.
CONNIE	I want someone I can take seriously.
ALBERT	What?
CONNIE	When I marry I want to marry someone nice.
ALBERT	Nice?
CONNIE	I wanna marry someone with prospects.
ALBERT	Prospects?
CONNIE	Someone who's gonna make something of himself.
ALBERT	I've got prospects.
CONNIE	I want someone who's exciting.
ALBERT	I'm exciting.
CONNIE	Someone who's really exciting to be with.

ALBERT   I'm dead exciting. There's nobody more exciting than me. (*He fishes in his pocket and pulls out an imaginary half crown.*) See that window, that's open? Look at that, there's half a crown. (*He throws it away.*)

CONNIE   Albert!

ALBERT   (*he folds his arms*) And I don't even care.

CONNIE   I wanna marry someone impulsive.

ALBERT   I booked sick yesterday.

CONNIE   I wouldn't marry you.

ALBERT   What's wrong with me?

CONNIE   You're not my type.

ALBERT   'Course I'm your type.

CONNIE   It wouldn't work.

ALBERT   'Course it would work.

CONNIE   Look. I'm not marrying you.

ALBERT   Why not?

CONNIE   Well you've never asked me, for one?

ALBERT   Will you marry me, for God's sake?

         (CONNIE *turns to the audience and smiles triumphantly. She looks back at* ALBERT.)

CONNIE   NO!

ALBERT   What do you mean no?

CONNIE   I mean no. You're not exciting you haven't gone down on one knee or 'owt.

         (ALBERT *goes down on one knee.*)

ALBERT   Will you marry me?

CONNIE   The room had filled with about forty people all wanting to buy a house.

         (*They look round grimacing with embarrassment.* ALBERT *forces out a half-laugh.*)

         They gave us a round of applause.

         (ALBERT *stands.*)

         You spent five hours looking for that half crown.

         (ALBERT *picks up his newspaper – the Daily Mail – and sits in his armchair.*)

ALBERT   I'm bloody sure I didn't. Eeh well, forty bloody years. Now I'm gonna enjoy meself.

CONNIE   Not if you have to spend money, you're not.

ALBERT   I'm ignoring you . . .

CONNIE   What're you gonna do every day?

ALBERT   Don't worry about me.

CONNIE   You haven't got any friends.

ALBERT   I'm alright.

CONNIE   You haven't got any hobbies.

ALBERT   I can look after meself.

CONNIE   You're not exactly Alan Whicker, are you?

ALBERT   Sod off.

CONNIE   Would you like me to introduce you to the washing machine?

ALBERT   I wondered how long it would be.

CONNIE   You wouldn't know where to start.

ALBERT   Can't I have one sodding day's peace?

CONNIE   You know what they call me at the sports centre? The Olympic Flame.

ALBERT   Why?

CONNIE   'Cos I never bloody go out. You even take the bin out once a week.

ALBERT   Do you want me to take you out, is that what you want?

    (ALBERT *leaves his newspaper on the armchiar and moves up left towards the kitchen.*)

CONNIE   Waiting on you hand and foot. Forty years of picking your shitty underpants up of the bedroom floor.

ALBERT   You're lucky it wasn't the ceiling.

    (*He exits.*)

CONNIE   How do you get them so shitty?

ALBERT   I'm ignoring you.

    (CONNIE *takes the newspaper from the armchair and puts it in the magazine rack, up left.*)

CONNIE   I'm gonna tell me mam. I'll tell her about the way you treat me.

ALBERT   (*off*) You can.

CONNIE   I am, don't you worry!

    (ALBERT *enters with a glass of water.*)

ALBERT   It won't do much good.

CONNIE   Why not?

    (ALBERT *takes his tablets.*)

ALBERT   She's been dead five years.

CONNIE   I can still talk to her.

ALBERT   You can't talk to the dead.

CONNIE   Why not? Give me one good reason why not?

          (*Pause.*)

ALBERT   (*spelling out the obvious*) 'Cos they're bloody
          dead.

CONNIE   I get more sense out of her than I do out of you.

ALBERT   You would do.

          (ALBERT *looks for the paper and, realising that*
          CONNIE *must have tidied it away, gives her a dirty*
          look before retrieving it from the magazine rack.)

CONNIE   Why do you have to drag me mother into it, you
          know how much I miss her.

ALBERT   Have I taken me tablets?

CONNIE   Yes.

ALBERT   I haven't.

CONNIE   I've just stood and watched you.

ALBERT   When?

CONNIE   Just then, you've just this minute taken them.

ALBERT   I haven't, ya' know.

CONNIE   (*shouting*) I've just bloody watched you.

ALBERT   (*shouting even louder*) There's no need to bloody
          shout.

          (ALBERT *is somewhat confused. He makes his way*
          to his armchair and sits.)

          Oh God. I'm getting old aren't I? I'm an *old age*
          pensioner.

CONNIE   And a miserable one at that.

ALBERT   I never ever saw meself as an old man.

CONNIE   Don't be so bloody stupid, you're not old.

          (*He stands and looks in the mirror, downstage
          right of centre.*)

ALBERT   I am. I mean I don't feel old. I don't feel much
          different, apart from a few aches an' that. But I've
          been thinking, you know, there's some things I'll
          never do again.

CONNIE   It's been that long you've probably forgotten.

ALBERT   I'll never play with worms again.

CONNIE   Worms.

ALBERT   As a little lad I used to love cutting up worms or
          riding down Eston Bank on me bogey. And I'll
          never go fishing for sticklebacks and redbreasts
          up Tinker's Alley . . . or . . . or play kick a tin or
          marbles.

CONNIE   Well you lost them years ago.

          (ALBERT *moves to the window downstage left of
          centre and looks out.*)

ALBERT   And I used to love kicking a ball in the street. I
          used to spend hours kicking a ball in the street.
          But I'll never do it anymore, I'll never have that
          feeling again, that rush of excitement you get 'cos
          I'm bloody old.

CONNIE   You are not old.

ALBERT   I am.

CONNIE   (*emphatic*) You're not. You've got loads of life in
          ya'.

ALBERT   Where's me football boots?

CONNIE   What?

ALBERT   Me football boots.

          (*He exits in search of his boots.*)

CONNIE	(*shouting after him*) What do you want them for?
ALBERT	'Cos I'm gonna have a game.
CONNIE	You're gonna have a game!
ALBERT	Where's me boots?
CONNIE	Be bloody sensible.
ALBERT	Me boots aren't here
CONNIE	Where?

(ALBERT *appears.*)

ALBERT	In the cupboard where I left 'em. I always keep 'em in the cupboard under the stairs.
CONNIE	You said you'd packed in.
ALBERT	Well I'm gonna start again. They must be here somewhere.

(ALBERT *goes to exit once more.*)

CONNIE	I threw 'em out.

(ALBERT *checks. And, like thunder, he slowly turns.*)

ALBERT	What?
CONNIE	I threw them out.
ALBERT	You threw em out!
CONNIE	You never used 'em.
ALBERT	You threw 'em out!
CONNIE	You packed in.
ALBERT	You threw me boots out.
CONNIE	You said you'd finished.
ALBERT	Me Adidas Santiagos.

CONNIE   You never used 'em.

ALBERT   They were bloody expensive.

CONNIE   Never touched 'em for years.

ALBERT   Do I touch your things? Do I . . . fiddle with your
            clothes? Do I throw your things out?

CONNIE   I didn't think you needed 'em.

ALBERT   Well I bloody do.

CONNIE   You packed in.

ALBERT   They're my boots.

CONNIE   You can't play now.

ALBERT   Why can't I?

CONNIE   (*shouting*) 'Cos your too bloody old!

            (*Silence. He looks at her for a moment and then
            hurt, he moves away towards the table, stage left.
            He stops, looks at* CONNIE *before defiantly moving
            the plant that is in the middle of the table. He sits
            at the table. She feels for him and talks with
            tenderness.*)

            Look, you'll be alright.

ALBERT   What's it all about, Con?

CONNIE   I'll tell you what it's all about, it's about you and
            me.

            (ALBERT *half-smiles.*)

ALBERT   I don't know what I'd've done without you.

CONNIE   I don't.

ALBERT   You've been good to me.

CONNIE   Don't I know it.

ALBERT   Stuck by me through all me moods and that. We
              do alright though don't we Con, we don't do bad.
              I mean we're normal, aren't we?

CONNIE   You're not bloody normal. (*Pause.*) But I wouldn't
              swap you.

              (*She joins him at the table. He turns to look at
              her. She speaks with affection.*)

              You're still a hell of a bloke, Albert Nobbs. Hey we
              could dance, couldn't we?

ALBERT   The bloody best.

CONNIE   Every Saturday in the Dock club.

ALBERT   They don't call it that now.

CONNIE   We used to clear the floor.

ALBERT   Yeah but those days are all gone, Con?

CONNIE   Bugger off, are they? (*Excited.*) Lets dance,
              Albert?

ALBERT   Give over!

CONNIE   (*moving to the CDs, up centre*) Oh come on, I'll
              put some Barry Manilow on.

ALBERT   Barry bloody Manilow!

CONNIE   You used to call me Lola when our Judith was
              little.

ALBERT   I would have called you Henry Cooper. I would
              have stuck my head between me legs and kissed
              me arse goodbye if meant getting me end aw –

CONNIE   Don't be so bloody vulgar.

ALBERT   Barry bloody Manilow.

CONNIE   Right, well we'll put some Frank on, then.

ALBERT   They should have him put down, Barry Manilow.

CONNIE   Come on, there's no one watching.

(She moves over to the CD player, up left.)

ALBERT   He's a bloody menace to society, Barry Manilow.

CONNIE   Come on.

ALBERT   The big-nose bugger.

CONNIE   Are you ready?

ALBERT   Give over.

CONNIE   Oh, come on.

ALBERT   I haven't had me morning constitutional.

(She puts a Frank Sinatra CD on, 'I Get a Kick Out of You'.)

CONNIE   Come on Albert, sweep me off me feet like you used to.

ALBERT   I'll not dance in me own front room on a Monday morning and that's final.

CONNIE   Alright then, there's a tea dance at the Finnegan's Hall on Thursday. I've always fancied that. Do you fancy going?

ALBERT   A tea dance. A bloody tea dance. You wanna go to a tea dance. I'd rather be dead.

CONNIE   That can be arranged.

ALBERT   A bloody tea dance.

CONNIE   Well what are you gonna do all day?

ALBERT   *(standing, contronting her)* I might have played football if I had some boots.

CONNIE   Well you're gonna have to do something.

ALBERT   I'll play me records.

CONNIE   Every day?

(*He moves to the arm chair, picks up his paper and turns towards her*).

ALBERT   What the hell is the matter with you? I am going to sit down here, read the paper, pick a few horses out and then I am going up stairs for a shit. And then in a couple of years time, I'm gonna die. Problem with that?

CONNIE   No.

ALBERT   Good. (*He sits down chuntering into the paper.*) Me first bloody day off and I can't get a minute's bloody peace.

          (CONNIE *switches off the CD.*)

          I was listening to that.

          (*Pause.* CONNIE *hovers, plucking up the courage to ask him something. She sits at the table. He looks up from the paper, she smiles at him. He grunts and returns to the paper.*)

CONNIE   Maybe we could go and visit our Judith.

ALBERT   She lives in New Zealand.

CONNIE   I know where she lives.

ALBERT   Oh well just a minute, I'll get me coat.

CONNIE   We've never been out there.

ALBERT   Do you know how much it costs?

CONNIE   Mandy's me only grandchild and I wanna see her.

ALBERT   There's a photograph of her over there, have a look at that.

CONNIE   It's 'cos you're scared of flying, isn't it?

ALBERT   (ALBERT *is terrified of flying*) No.

CONNIE   You are.

ALBERT	It's me cholestrol.
CONNIE	You big soft bugger.
ALBERT	And I'm on Warfarin.
CONNIE	Scared of going in a little aeroplane.
ALBERT	It's me condition.
CONNIE	You had a funny turn in Binns' lift.
ALBERT	I'm bloody ill you daft bugger, you ask the doctor. I'd love to go, I'd go tomorrow, he just won't let me.
CONNIE	You can't relax, that's your trouble.
ALBERT	I never get a bloody chance.
CONNIE	(*making her way to the cupboard, up centre*) No, and you'll have less in a minute 'cos Rose's coming round for a reading.
ALBERT	Bloody hell! I thought you'd packed all that rubbish in.
	(CONNIE *takes out a crystal ball wrapped in velvet and walks to the table, left.*)
CONNIE	Well I have – and it's not rubbish. Rose begged me to and I said I would. And you be nice to her.
ALBERT	What you talking about, I've got a soft spot for her.
CONNIE	Yeah, right.
ALBERT	It's a swamp in Florida.
CONNIE	I'm warning you.
ALBERT	Well if she calls me Alby just once so help me I'm gonna bloody swing for her.
ROSE	(*from off-stage*) Anybody there?
ALBERT	(*shouting*) No, we're out.

CONNIE   Albert.

                (ROSE *appears*.)

ROSE   Alright Connie?

CONNIE   I'll take your coat.

ALBERT   Funny, I never heard you knock.

                (CONNIE *takes* ROSE'S *coat and hangs it on a hook, up right.*)

CONNIE   I'm warning you.

ROSE   Here he is, how you feeling, Alby?

ALBERT   Albert.

                (CONNIE *moves to the table and wipes the crystal ball in preparation for the reading.*)

ROSE   First day off! He looks good on it, doesn't he? Doesn't he look good on it? (*To* ALBERT.) Eeeeh, who'd a thought it.

ALBERT   Aye.

ROSE   You don't look any different or owt.

ALBERT   Don't I?

ROSE   You look just the same.

ALBERT   Go on.

ROSE   He looks just the same.

                (ALBERT *smiles at* ROSE *and glares at* CONNIE.)

                First day of freedom. It'll take a bit of time to get used to it.

ALBERT   It will if you keep popping in.

CONNIE   Ignore him!

ROSE   Well I've got a couple of things need doing if you get bored. Me bush is desperate for a bit of attention. I used to see to it meself but it's too strenuous now.

CONNIE   You've got a lovely bush.

ROSE   Everyone says that. People used to make a special journey to see my bush.

ALBERT   (*rhetorically*) Is it me?

CONNIE   Albert! Rose wants you to have a look at her bush.

            (ALBERT *looks up and attempts a little laugh that comes out as a pathetic whimper.*)

            (*insistent*) Will you sort out her bush?

ALBERT   I dare say I could have a good look at it for her.

ROSE   It needs a man's hand now.

            (ALBERT *smiles at* ROSE *and then gives* CONNIE *a knowing look.*)

            You have to keep busy. Peter Burke up the road, hung himself the day after he finished.

CONNIE   He did.

ROSE   He was found, the day after he finished, swinging from the loft.

CONNIE   He was.

ALBERT   Had you been round to visit him?

CONNIE   Albert!

ROSE   Tommy Graham lasted three months.

CONNIE   Albert's not been well.

ALBERT   Bloody hell!

ROSE   I'd get him checked out.

CONNIE	He won't go to the doctors.
ROSE	Is it his cholesterol?
CONNIE	Crippled with pain he is, some days.
ROSE	Arthur Coyle was like that and you know what happened to him.
CONNIE	Dead within the month.
ALBERT	Have you finished?
ROSE	Well, what you gonna do all day?
CONNIE	He's too bloody miserable to enjoy himself.
ALBERT	I wish I was back at bloody work.
CONNIE	Maybe it would be better if we left it for today.
ROSE	You promised, and I've been looking forward to it. Oh, come on . . .
CONNIE	All right. (*Turning to* ALBERT.) Look I think it would be better if you went out.
ALBERT	Went out!
CONNIE	Just for half an hour.
ALBERT	You want me to go out.
CONNIE	We won't be long.
ALBERT	You want me to go out on me first day off.
CONNIE	Don't be awkward.
ALBERT	Bugger off. This is my bloody house so you can shit. Go out!
CONNIE	I don't think this is going to work.
ALBERT	(*chuntering to himself*) Me own bloody house . . .
ROSE	Oh Connie, you can't do this to me now, I'm desperate.

ALBERT   (*to himself*) You're not bloody kidding.

CONNIE   But I haven't done anything like this for ages.

ROSE   But I've been looking forward to it.

ALBERT   Bloody go out!

CONNIE   Right, well, come on then. (*To* ALBERT.) You better behave yourself.

ALBERT   I haven't said a word.

CONNIE   I'm warning you –

ALBERT   I'm reading the paper.

(*They sit at a table.* CONNIE *hands* ROSE *the crystal ball.*)

CONNIE   Hold that.

ALBERT   Bloody go out!

CONNIE   You have to concentrate.

ROSE   I'm concentrating.

(CONNIE *places a transparent veil over her head and stares at the crystal ball.*)

ALBERT   Good God.

ROSE   (*to* ALBERT) Ssssh! (*To* CONNIE.) Is there anything happening?

CONNIE   Ssssh.

(*Small pause.*)

ROSE   Are you getting anything?

ALBERT   (*mocking, as a ghost*) Oooooooh.

CONNIE   Right, that's it.

ROSE   Albert!

ALBERT   What?

CONNIE   You had to do it, didn't you?

ALBERT   I'm reading the paper.

CONNIE   You think you're bloody clever. (*To* ROSE.) It's no good.

ROSE   Please! (*To* ALBERT.) Bloody shut it.

ALBERT   I've not said a word.

ROSE   Come on, just one more try, please.

Connie   (*she starts to get something coming through*)
              Hang on a minute . . .

ROSE   What? What?

CONNIE   I'm getting something . . .

ROSE   She's getting something.

ALBERT   It's probably a headache.

CONNIE   Oh, it's gone.

ROSE   What?

CONNIE   It's gone.

ROSE   Well try again!

CONNIE   No, it's gone.

ROSE   You must be able to get it back. Look closer. There must be something in there.

CONNIE   (*clearing things away*) There was too many interruptions. (*Pointed.*) There's a strong negative force in the room.

              (*They both turn and look at* ALBERT. ALBERT, *aware of their stares, looks up from the paper.*)

ALBERT   I'm reading the bloody paper.

ROSE   I bet it was a man. Do you think it could have been a man?

CONNIE   It could have been.

ROSE   I knew it. I knew it was a man. Did you hear that, there's romance ahead. I knew it. (*Teasing*.) I bet it's Albert.

           (CONNIE *gets her sports bag up right, and checks its contents on the table.*)

ALBERT   I bet it's bloody not!

ROSE   Give over, you fancy me.

CONNIE   Course he does.

ROSE   Finds me desirable.

CONNIE   He's just playing hard-to-get.

ROSE   (*checking herself in the mirror*) Albert, be serious, am I the kind of woman you would go for?

ALBERT   Only with a carving knife.

CONNIE   He'd run a bloody mile. He needs a week's notice to build himself up for it.

ALBERT   Have you finished?

CONNIE   And his eyesight's not what it was.

ROSE   I could lend you a hand, Albert.

CONNIE   You need to, 'cos he can't put it in on his own.

           (ROSE *and* CONNIE *laugh.*)

ROSE   I bet he's a right little sex god when he gets going.

ALBERT   I'd rather have a pork chop.

CONNIE   He's not bloody kidding either. (*Collecting their coats.*) Come on, we'd better get going.

ROSE   That instructor's been giving me the eye. Hey, I
            bet it's him!

ALBERT   Where you goin', dancin'?

CONNIE   We've not been dancing for months.

ROSE   It's bums and tums on a Monday.

ALBERT   I thought it was wash day on a Monday.

            (CONNIE *and* ROSE *exchange a look.*)

CONNIE   (*to* ROSE) Don't.

ALBERT   Well, what about food?

CONNIE   We'll get something there. And don't forget to
            put the bin out.

ALBERT   How long you're gonna be?

CONNIE   He can't bear to have me out of his sight.

ROSE   Well come on, young men beckon.

ALBERT   Bloody hell.

ROSE   See you, sexy.

            (CONNIE *and* ROSE *sing as they exit, 'Kiss Me Once
            and Kiss Me Twice and Kiss Me Once Again'.*)

            See you, Alby.

            (*They exit, up left.*)

ALBERT   (*throwing his paper in their direction*) Bloody
            women!

            (*Music in, 'Love and Marriage'.*)

            Forty years for this. Forty bloody years. Have I
            taken me tablets?

            (*Blackout.*)

Scene Three

ALBERT *sits transfixed, staring at the wall.* CONNIE *enters, carrying an empty shopping bag, notices* ALBERT *then addresses the audience. Music out.*

CONNIE   Albert and retirement haven't really settled in well.

ALBERT   There's eight hundred and thirty seven flowers on that wall alone.

CONNIE   Is there? (*Aside.*) He's driving me mad.

ALBERT   And one thousand two hundred and twenty three leaves. Where you going?

CONNIE   I've got a bit of shopping to do.

ALBERT   You went shopping yesterday. We've been married twenty years.

CONNIE   Thirty-five.

ALBERT   (*pause*) Well you've spent thirty-two of 'em shopping. (ALBERT *throws down the paper and makes his way to the window*.) Hey! He's at it again. (*He runs outside.*) What's my privet ever done to you? Now just bugger off and play up your own end. (*Pause.*) If that ball comes on my garden, I'll put a bloody knife through it. Do you hear me? A bloody knife through it.

CHILD'S   (*off*) Fuck off, you old git.
VOICE

ALBERT   What? Hey! I know where you live. I know where you live.

(ALBERT *re-enters the house.*)

Did you hear that? Did you hear what he said to me?

CONNIE   You wanna calm down.

ALBERT   They ought to bring back hanging.

CONNIE   Calm down.

ALBERT   They never play up their own end. They always
            have to play outside our house.

CONNIE   Oh, for Heaven's sake.

            (ALBERT *chunters as he sits at the table.*)

ALBERT   They've got no bloody respect kids these days.
            They ought to bring back the birch, that'd bloody
            fettle 'em.

CONNIE   (*she composes herself and joins* ALBERT *at the
            table*) Look Albert, listen . . . I think you need to
            get away on a holiday. Have a break, spend a
            couple of weeks in the sun and then come back
            nice and refreshed.

ALBERT   I'd feel guilty leaving you here on your own.

CONNIE   I'm coming with you, you daft sod. You don't
            think I'd send you off on your own without me do
            you?

ALBERT   No, of course not.

CONNIE   I thought maybe we could go and see our Judith in
            New Zealand.

ALBERT   So that's what this is about.

            (*He moves away.*)

CONNIE   I want to see our Mandy. She'll grow up and she
            won't even know who I am. She's me only grand
            child and she won't even know who I am.

            (*He drops the newspaper on the armchair and
            stands, right.*)

ALBERT   I'm not going through this again.

CONNIE   You've always been the same. You've always
            hated holidays.

ALBERT   It's going with you that puts me off.

CONNIE   It was the same on our first holiday. You were bloody terrified of eating anything . . .

ALBERT   I don't like spicy food.

(CONNIE *moves from the table to comfort* ALBERT, *stage right.*)

CONNIE   His suitcase was packed with Ringtons tea bags, Newboulds pies, sugar, milk, coffee, coffee mate, bacon, sausages three boxes of Sugar Puffs and thiry-five tins of baked beans.

ALBERT   I'm not eating any of that foreign rubbish.

CONNIE   We were only going to Scarborough for a week in a caravan.

(*The lights fade to a small area, stage right. Sound of seagulls.*)

It's small, isn't it?

ALBERT   Where do I sleep?

CONNIE   There I think.

ALBERT   They're having a bloody laugh, aren't they?

CONNIE   It'll be alright.

ALBERT   I'll have to sleep bent double.

CONNIE   It's supposed to sleep a family of six.

ALBERT   It would do if they were pigmies.

CONNIE   You'll manage.

ALBERT   I'm not a bloody contortionist. Look, I can't sleep with me knees up my nostril, it doesn't work.

CONNIE   Right, well we'll sleep in that hotel on the front.

ALBERT   Are you out of your mind? Do you know how much it costs for a week in one of them places?

CONNIE   Well this is my holiday and I'm determined to have
            a good time even if it kills me.

ALBERT   But they cost a fortune.

CONNIE   Whole families sleep in caravans.

ALBERT   You need a mortgage to stay in one of them!

CONNIE   Well I'll tell you something for nothing, I'm not
            having a family with you, so you can shit.

ALBERT   But they cost twenty pounds a week.

CONNIE   Shit, Albert!

ALBERT   Happy bloody holiday!

CONNIE   Can you imagine a family on holiday with you?

ALBERT   What's the matter with me?

CONNIE   You're bloody useless.

ALBERT   Who is?

CONNIE   You!

ALBERT   Hey, I'm good with kids.

CONNIE   Huh?

ALBERT   They love me. They find me funny.

CONNIE   I don't know how.

ALBERT   I'd be over that park with the ball.

CONNIE   You'd be too busy working.

ALBERT   I'm dying for kids.

CONNIE   Rubbish!

ALBERT   I'd love a family.

CONNIE   You'd shit yourself.

ALBERT   I'm looking forward to it.

CONNIE   You'd run a bloody mile.

ALBERT   The sooner the better as far as I'm concerned.

CONNIE   Well you're gonna have a long wait.

          (*An idea flashes into his head.*)

ALBERT   We'll start now.

CONNIE   We bloody won't.

ALBERT   No, bugger, it we'll christen the bloody caravan.

CONNIE   We will not.

ALBERT   Come on.

CONNIE   Don't you dare touch me.

ALBERT   Come on, I want a family.

CONNIE   Keep off me!

ALBERT   Why?

CONNIE   'Cos I'm pregnant.

          (*Pause.*)

ALBERT   Rubbish.

          (*Silence.*)

CONNIE   Three months.

ALBERT   What? No!

          (*She nods.*)

          Are you sure it's yours? Hey sit down. You
          shouldn't be stood up.

CONNIE   I'm okay.

ALBERT   You can't be too careful.

CONNIE   Albert, I'm alright! I'm fine.

ALBERT   Connie, I'm gonna be a dad.

CONNIE   Yeah.

            (*Pause.*)

ALBERT   A bloody dad!

CONNIE   Yeah.

            (*Pause.*)

ALBERT   And . . . you, you'll be a mam.

CONNIE   That's right.

ALBERT   I'll be a dad and you'll be a mam.

CONNIE   Well I'm pleased we've got that sorted out.

ALBERT   Oh God!

            (*Pause. Silence.*)

CONNIE   Are you okay?

ALBERT   Yeah.

CONNIE   Are you crying?

ALBERT   No!

CONNIE   You are, you're bloody crying.

ALBERT   I can't bloody help it.

CONNIE   You soft bugger.

ALBERT   There's nowt wrong with crying. It doesn't make
            you a small man.

CONNIE   Here.

            (*She offers him a tissue. He repels her offer.*)

ALBERT   Bugger off. Caravan! Bugger this for a game of soldiers.

CONNIE   Where you going?

ALBERT   I'm gonna book in that hotel on the front.

          (*Lights rise on the room.*)

CONNIE   And we did. A beautiful three star hotel.

ALBERT   You could see two of them through the roof.

          (ALBERT *sits in his armchair.*)

CONNIE   I felt like a queen.

ALBERT   I felt like we'd been done.

CONNIE   We had a good time though, didn't we?

ALBERT   (*stern and miserable*) I'm a good laugh.

CONNIE   Heaven preserve us . . .

          (CONNIE *moves back into the room, centre.*)

          Let's do it Albert, New Zealand would be brilliant.

ALBERT   We'll go next year.

CONNIE   But you said that last year.

ALBERT   I've only been retired a month.

CONNIE   I think about her every day.

ALBERT   I'm ignoring you.

CONNIE   You can pretend to be heartless, but I know you. It was the same the first day we took her to university.

ALBERT   Where's all this come from?

CONNIE   We dropped her off at university and then got back home. And you were pretending you weren't bothered, but I could tell. (*To the audience*.) He started whistling.

(ALBERT *starts whistling a Frank Sinatra tune*.)

CONNIE   Well that's it, then.

(*She sits at the table*.)

ALBERT   Yeah.

CONNIE   She's gone.

ALBERT   Yeah.

(ALBERT *pours two very large whiskies*.)

CONNIE   I miss her.

ALBERT   She's only been gone two hours.

CONNIE   I can't help it.

(ALBERT *offers* CONNIE *her whisky. It's enormous. She looks at it*.)

Albert!

ALBERT   Bloody drink it.

CONNIE   The house feels empty.

ALBERT   I think I'll go an introduce meself to the bathroom.

CONNIE   She won't come back, ya know.

ALBERT   I suppose we'll just have to bloody talk to each other.

CONNIE   No, she's flown the nest. That's it now. Once they've gone, they never really come back.

ALBERT   Wha . . . wha . . . what the hell you talking about?

CONNIE   She'll meet someone at university or she'll stay down there or she'll go straight into her own job and she'll buy her own house.

ALBERT   Don't ..don't. be so bloody stupid. (ALBERT *finishes his whisky and replenishes the glass.*) It's 'cos you've been too bloody soft with her.

CONNIE   If I'd realised twenty years ago when she was born that I had to give her away again, I don't think I would have had her.

ALBERT   For God's sake.

CONNIE   She's a good kid, isn't she? I mean she can look after herself, can't she? I mean we've done well, haven't we. She's dead popular, everyone says so.

ALBERT   (*stern*) She gets that from me.

    (*Pause.* ALBERT *finishes his glass.* CONNIE *gets upset.*)

CONNIE   She doesn't need me anymore. She used to need me. And now she doesn't.

ALBERT   Hey, come on . . .

CONNIE   She used to be my little girl and now she doesn't need me. What am I going to do, Albert?

ALBERT   (*joining her at the table*) 'Course she bloody needs you, you're her mam and you'll always be her mam.

CONNIE   What have I got to look forward to? And she's so far away. I'll never see her.

ALBERT   She's only gone to Leeds.

CONNIE   I feel as though a part of me has died.

ALBERT   University is right for her. She gets her brains from me. We never had those opportunities and you wouldn't want to deprive her of them, would you?

    (*The phone rings. They both freeze like rabbits in the headlights.* CONNIE *dashes for the phone.*)

CONNIE   Hello. (*Pause*.) Hello Judith. Oh Judith, it's good
            to hear your voice . . . yes we got home alright
            thanks, Judith. (*She puts her hand over the
            mouthpiece*.) It's Judith.

            (ALBERT *looks disgusted*.)

            Don't be silly, course I won't touch your room.
            Hey, what's up? What's the matter? Now come on.
            No, look don't cry. Don't cry. (*She puts her hand
            over the mouthpiece*.) She's crying. (*Into phone*.)
            Look, it'll be alright. You'll be alright tomorrow.

ALBERT   Let me speak.

CONNIE   You'll meet loads of new people.

ALBERT   Let me speak.

CONNIE   Your dad wants a word. (*To* ALBERT.) She's hung
            up.

ALBERT   Oh bloody hell! (*He finishes his whisky and goes
            to pour himself another one.* CONNIE *starts to ring
            her back*.) This is your bloody fault, this.

CONNIE   Mine!

ALBERT   Bloody university . . .

CONNIE   What?

ALBERT   What the hell does she wanna go there for?

CONNIE   I'll ring her back.

ALBERT   We never went to university and it didn't do us
            any harm. She should be home where we can look
            after her. No bugger it, I'll go and get her. She can
            go next year.

CONNIE   It's ringing.

ALBERT   Let me talk.

CONNIE   Get off.

ALBERT	Tell her I'm coming for her.
CONNIE	She's not answering.
ALBERT	Where's the car keys?
CONNIE	Albert! Albert! You're going nowhere. You've had too much to drink.

(CONNIE *puts the receiver down.*)

ALBERT	I've had one little whisky.
CONNIE	Look, she'll be fine. She's bound to feel strange.

(ALBERT *pours himself another whisky.*)

ALBERT	I could bloody scream, I could.
CONNIE	How do you think I feel?

(CONNIE *takes the bottle and helps herself to another whisky.*)

ALBERT	She's gonna be sat in that poky little room on her own, crying her bloody eyes out.
CONNIE	Don't. Bloody hell, don't. I can't stand it.
ALBERT	If anything happens to her I'll bloody kill you.
CONNIE	Me?
ALBERT	Yes you.
CONNIE	Shit, Albert.
ALBERT	You shit.

(*They both down their whiskies in one and simultaneously slam down their glasses on the unit, up centre.*)

CONNIE	We got drunk that night.
ALBERT	Drank a whole bottle of whisky.
CONNIE	And she never did come back, did she?

ALBERT   No, no she didn't.

CONNIE   Well, let's go and see her.

ALBERT   (*sitting in his armchair*) We'll book for next year.
             Bloody hell, I've only been retired a month.

CONNIE   And it seems like a bloody year. Right, well,
             you're gonna have to do something 'cos you're
             driving me up the bloody wall.

ALBERT   I'm ignoring you.

CONNIE   Do you wanna go for a walk?

             (ALBERT *is horrified.*)

ALBERT   A walk! A bloody walk! What the hell do you
             wanna go on a walk for? We've got a car.

CONNIE   A bit of fresh air.

ALBERT   I've got some fresh air, I stood on the step this
             morning.

CONNIE   We used to go on walks, when we were courting.
             You walked miles to see me when we were
             courting.

ALBERT   A bloody walk.

CONNIE   You used to fancy me then.

ALBERT   You had sommat to fancy.

CONNIE   Don't you fancy me now?

ALBERT   I'm still with you, aren't I?

CONNIE   When you look at me, what do you see?

             (ALBERT *looks at her.*)

ALBERT   Jordan.

CONNIE   Why can't you be serious?

ALBERT   Well you started it.

CONNIE   Do you fancy going upstairs?

          (ALBERT *looks shocked.*)

ALBERT   What for?

CONNIE   (*suggestive*) You know.

ALBERT   It's not Saturday, is it?

CONNIE   You used to be so impulsive.

ALBERT   And look where it's got me.

          (CONNIE *goes and attempts to put her arms round him.*)

CONNIE   You don't fancy me any more, do ya?

ALBERT   Give over.

CONNIE   We never –

ALBERT   Connie!

CONNIE   Come on.

ALBERT   Gerrroofff.

CONNIE   Come on.

ALBERT   I've just had me breakfast.

          (*He gets up and moves to the table, left.*)

CONNIE   So? (*Slight pause.*) I'll dress up for you.

ALBERT   I've just had me cornflakes. Shurrrup.

CONNIE   (*going to put her arms around him*) You know you want to.

ALBERT   (*emphatic*) No, I bloody don't want to.

CONNIE   Well bugger you, then.

ALBERT   I'm sure God's a woman.

CONNIE	What?
ALBERT	It's only a woman that would put me through this living hell.
CONNIE	Listen, if God was a woman, sperm would taste of chocolate.
ALBERT	Connie, that is disgusting.
CONNIE	Well you've never been romantic.
ALBERT	Who hasn't.
CONNIE	And as for sex . . .
ALBERT	I've taken you to heaven and back.
CONNIE	Huh! Your idea of foreplay is spitting on your hands and shouting, 'Brace yourself'.
ALBERT	I'm ignoring you.
CONNIE	Let me tell you this, people fancy me.
ALBERT	Right, oh!
CONNIE	People still find me attractive. In fact I was propositioned last week.
ALBERT	I'm ignor – what?
CONNIE	On a date.
ALBERT	Bugger off.
CONNIE	Nice he was, an' all.
ALBERT	You're making it up.
CONNIE	Am I?
ALBERT	Who was he?
CONNIE	Sexy, he was.
ALBERT	Bloody sexy!

CONNIE	Asked me out.
ALBERT	He what?
CONNIE	Asked me out.
ALBERT	Bugger off.
CONNIE	Handsome, he was.
ALBERT	Right, come on then.

(ALBERT *starts to rip off his clothes.*)

CONNIE	Albert!
ALBERT	You asked for it.
CONNIE	Albert!
ALBERT	I'll give you sexy . . .
CONNIE	What are you doin'?
ALBERT	The full monty!
CONNIE	Albert!
ALBERT	I'll give you bloody sexy.
CONNIE	What if someone comes in?
ALBERT	They'll get a pleasant surprise. No, bugger it, if you want sexy I'll give you bloody sexy.

(ALBERT *has stripped down to his underpants, shoes and socks.* CONNIE *looks him up and down.*)

ALBERT	Right, then.
CONNIE	Yeah, I see what you mean. I bet Richard Gere's shitting himself.
ALBERT	Come here you . . . you . . . vixen!
CONNIE	Albert, no.

(He chases her round the room.)

CONNIE   Albert, no!

ALBERT   Come here!

CONNIE   Albert, you'll hurt yourself.

ALBERT   You asked for it.

CONNIE   Your cholesterol.

(He catches her, throws her on the armchair and climbs on top of her.)

Bloody hell, Albert! Albert. Be bloody gentle.

(ALBERT *is now laying on top of* CONNIE. *He jerks his body and screams out.*)

ALBERT   Oh my God!

CONNIE   You've haven't come already?

ALBERT   Oh!

CONNIE   What?

ALBERT   Bloody hell!

CONNIE   What?

ALBERT   I think I've put me back out.

CONNIE   What?

ALBERT   It's me back.

CONNIE   Well, keep still.

ALBERT   (*shouting*) I can't bloody move!

CONNIE   Let me rub it for you.

ALBERT   Careful.

CONNIE   Keep still!

ALBERT   Shit, Connie!

CONNIE   What's that like?

ALBERT   Lower. (*He groans.*)

CONNIE   How's that?

ALBERT   Ooh, that's nice. Oooh, that's lovely.

CONNIE   Keep still.

ALBERT   Keep going.

(ROSE *enters and watches.*)

Don't stop. Ooh yes! Oh yes, that's lovely. Oh
that's gorgeous. Oh, that's nice. Oh that is nice.
Oh, that is fantastic.

(ROSE *gives a little cough.*)

ROSE   Don't mind me.

(CONNIE *throws* ALBERT *off. He screams in
absolute agony. He clambers to his feet and
stands at a forty-five degree angle.*)

CONNIE   Hello, Rose.

ALBERT   Don't you ever knock?

ROSE   Not as often as you by the look of it. (*A pause.*)
You don't have to stand to attention for me.

(ALBERT *looks down at his genitals and then
covers them with both hands and groans as he
does so.*)

CONNIE   He won't leave me alone.

ALBERT   Bugger off!

ROSE   Right, well I'll better going then. I'll go on
without you. (*Pause – she turns to face them once
more.*) I'll just tell him you're coming.

CONNIE   I'm bloody not.

ROSE	'Bye, Alby.

(ROSE *exits.* ALBERT *attempts to dress. He is in agony the whole time.*)

ALBERT	Bugger off. You knew she was coming.

CONNIE	At least someone was.

ALBERT	You did that on purpose!

CONNIE	Please!

ALBERT	Just to bloody embarrass me.

CONNIE	You don't need me for that. Look at the state of you. What are you doing wearing underwear like that?

ALBERT	They're comfortable.

CONNIE	Comfortable! You're a bloody slob.

ALBERT	Are you wearin' 'em?

CONNIE	You need to smarten yourself up a bit, you're a bloody disgrace.

ALBERT	Look don't talk to me. You selfish, spoilt little . . . little . . . swine.

CONNIE	How dare you! You're bloody lucky you've got me. 'Cos I'll tell you this, no bugger else would have you. You're a bad tempered miserable old bugger. (*Slight pause.*) And you're fat.

(ALBERT *noticeably breathes in.*)

ALBERT	What?

CONNIE	Big fat pig.

ALBERT	I'm not standing for this.

CONNIE	Well what you gonna do about it?

ALBERT	I'm . . . I'm going for a walk.

CONNIE   Well I won't be here when you get back.

ALBERT   Fine by me, you . . . you arsehole.

(CONNIE *gasps, shocked at the severity of the insult*.)

CONNIE   Right, that's it.

ALBERT   Where are you going?

CONNIE   Out. And I'm not coming back.

ALBERT   I'm ignoring you.

CONNIE   I hope I never see you again as long as I live.

ALBERT   Good. (*Small pause – shouting after her as she storms out*.) What am I going to do for me tea?

(*Music, Frank Sinatra's 'Makin' Whoopee'. Blackout.*)

Scene Four

Music out. ALBERT *sits in a chair staring out ahead, motionless.* CONNIE *enters slowly and stands in a pool of light, left.*

CONNIE   And I never saw him again. Joy rider. Said he swerved to avoid a black cat and ran straight into me. I knew retirement was slowly beginning to strangle him. And now this. I know people might think he's a miserable cantankerous old git – well he is. But I knew he loved me. I knew I meant a lot to him. The night I died he got into bed and laid next to me. And every night since he's taken my nighty out of the wardrobe and carefully laid it in the bed where I used to lay. He then gets in next to it and cuddles it. You know he never bloody cuddled me when I was alive but he cuddles my nighty. He's cuddled my nighty every night since I've been gone.

ALBERT   Goodnight, Connie.

CONNIE   Goodnight, Albert.

                (CONNIE *exits, slowly.* ALBERT *sits in his chair*
                staring out of the window. ROSE *enters. Music*
                out.)

ROSE   Albert, are you alright. Albert! Albert, what did
                the doctor say?

                (ALBERT *transfixed, doesn't acknowledge* ROSE
                but speaks staring straight ahead.)

ALBERT   He's given me tablets.

ROSE   What kind of tablets?

                (*He looks at her, worried.*)

ALBERT   He said I have to take them for the rest of my life.

Rose   (*reassuring*) Well that's nowt to worry about.
                Lots of people have to take tablets and they live
                to a ripe old age.

ALBERT   Yeah, but he's only given me four.

ROSE   You daft bugger.

                (*Silence.*)

ALBERT   I just keep seeing her there.

ROSE   Don't.

ALBERT   Laid on the pavement between Whatever U Want
                and Poundstretcher.

ROSE   Hey, come on.

ALBERT   I wish I knew where I was going to die.

ROSE   Why?

ALBERT   I wouldn't go there.

                (*Pause.*)

ROSE   Can I get you a cup of tea? Have you eaten? I'm
                gonna fix you something to eat.

                (ROSE *exits*.)

ALBERT   He's still alive. Walked away scot-free. Is that
                right? I ask you. I'd love to get my hands on him.
                Just give me ten minutes. That's all I want. Ten
                minutes.

ROSE   (*re-entering*) There's nothing in.

ALBERT   I've eaten it all.

ROSE   Look Albert, you can't go on like this. I'm here to
                help. If there's anything you want you've just got
                to ask . . . it's no trouble . . . it's no trouble at all.
                It's been a month now, and . . . well, you can't
                just sit there.

                (*Silence*.)

ALBERT   I'm gonna start decorating. Get rid of those
                bloody flowers. And a new carpet. That's it, that's
                what Connie wants. She's been wanting a new
                carpet now for years. Yeah, well she can have one.
                By bloody hell she can. Nothing is too good for
                her. And that patio she's been after. I was gonna
                do it meself but there's no point in killing yourself
                is there . . . no, I'll get some landscape gardeners
                in. Connie will like that. Wilkinson's, they're the
                best. Nothing but the best for my Connie. And I'm
                gonna get rid of this furniture, bugger it. It's old.
                We are not gonna sit on old furniture. No, we are
                gonna start living. What's the point in saving
                your money? Answer me that? No point, and
                that's why we are gonna spend it. That's what
                we're gonna do. We're gonna spend it. Live for
                today, that's my motto. We are going to have the
                best of everything . . . the best of . . . (*He catches
                his breath*.) the best of everything . . . you mark
                my words . . .

                (*He catches his breath and fights back the sobs,
                but to no avail*.)

ROSE   Oh, Albert!

              (ROSE *cuddles him.*)

ALBERT   What you doing? What do you think you're
              doing?

ROSE   I was trying to com –

ALBERT   We don't need you. We're gonna be alright on our
              own.

ROSE   Albert, please don't.

ALBERT   So you can bugger off, you interfering little shit.
              Go on. Go.

              (*He pushes her towards the exit.*)

ROSE   I loved her as well.

ALBERT   *Out!* Go on, get out.

ROSE   She was my best friend..

ALBERT   *And don't come back. We don't need you!*

              (*Pause. He pours himself a whisky.*)

              We're gonna be alright together. We don't need
              anybody. It's just you and me now, Connie. You
              and me. Like it's always been. And we're gonna
              live a bit. I've got money and we're gonna spend
              it, Con. By hell we are.

              (ALBERT *starts to sing the opening of 'The Tender
              Trap'.*)

              You see a pair of laughing eyes
              And suddenly you're sighing sighs
              You're thinking nothing's wrong
              You string along boy then snap

              (*Frank Sinatra's version takes over. Lights
              slowly fade down but not out.*)

              ....

(*Lights fade up.* ALBERT *takes* CONNIE'S *crystal ball and delicately places it on the table. He wipes his hands on his trousers and steals himself. He sits down and prepares himself. He puts on the veil and then talks into the crystal ball. Music fades out.*)

ALBERT   Connie, are you there? (*Pause.*) Come in Connie. (*Pause.*) This is Albert Nobbs calling Connie, come in. (*Pause.*) Connie if you are there, give me a sign. (*He listens and hears nothing. He sighs. Pause.*) What colour do you want the hall? Do you want Axminster or shaggy pile? Connie, for God's sake. Bloody hell! Bollocks! Look, I know I've been a tight miserable bastard but we had some good times didn't we. Oh shit!

(*Music in, Frank Sinatra's 'Dancing in the Dark'. ALBERT gets up from the table and pours himself a whisky. He notices his tablets and picks them up. He moves down and sits, then empties the contents of the bottle into his hand. CONNIE enters from stage left and stands in a pool of light, up left. Music fades out as ALBERT prepares to take all the tablets.*)

CONNIE   Are you alright, Albert?

ALBERT   Bloody hell, I nearly died then, you stupid bugger. Bugger me!

(*Blackout. Music in, Frank Sinatra's 'Witchcraft'. End of Act One.*)

ACT TWO

Scene One

ALBERT *is transfixed upstage.* CONNIE *stands downstage centre.*

CONNIE   It doesn't happen every day, does it?

ALBERT   (*still and staring*) Bloody hell.

CONNIE   He came round, fainted again, then he had his tablets, ranted and raved, popped another tablet under his tongue and then eventually he started to calm down.

               (*He walks slowly round her amazed, exclaiming as he goes.*)

ALBERT   Bloody hell!

CONNIE   Is that all you can say?

ALBERT   Bloody hell! Bloody hell. (*Pause.*) Shouldn't you have wings an' stuff?

CONNIE   Albert!

ALBERT   Bloody hell.

CONNIE   And you said *Ghost* was far-fetched?

ALBERT   Have you . . . you know . . . have you seen God?

CONNIE   Stop it.

ALBERT   What does he look like?

CONNIE   I'm worried about you.

ALBERT   Does he look like he does in the pictures?

CONNIE   Albert!

ALBERT   Does he walk round like spreading goodness everywhere? Does he have like Miracle of the Week an' that? Has he got an orchestra with strings an' that that follow him round?

CONNIE   Albert, that's enough.

ALBERT   'Cos he does sod-all down here. I've spent all my life, you know, eating Flora Lite, doing without sugar on me Weetabix, having sweeteners in me tea and struggling and saving to make ends meet. And for what? 'Cos I'll tell ya this for nowt, all I've got to look forward to is someone wiping me arse, dying of cancer, or losing me marbles. That's all. 'Cos that's what happens to us all. Or worse I could end up in some shitty nursing home with a party hat on holding a balloon while some do-good . . . community artist organises a singalong of, 'Lets all sing like the bloody birdy's sing'. And who'll care? No one. No one'll care about me.

      (*Pause.*)

CONNIE   You're just a bit down.

      (*He looks at her.*)

ALBERT   Down? Me? No. I think I'm gonna have a party. (*Shouting.*). Don't bother bringing any drink, I've got the spirit in. (*Pause – he looks into her eye.*) Why did you go and leave me?

CONNIE   I didn't exactly plan it.

ALBERT   You spent half your life looking into the future.

CONNIE   It was a car crash.

      (*He holds out the palm of his hand.*)

ALBERT   Owee then, tell me what's in store for me.

      (*She ignores it.*)

CONNIE   You're gonna be alright.

ALBERT   Alright. All . . . bloody right. Bloody brilliant. Forty years of hard graft, and then you come walking in like Demi Moore and –

CONNIE   Patrick Swayze.

ALBERT   Does it bloody matter? Come walking back in and
              tell me I'm gonna be all-bloody-right. You know, I
              wish I was back at work, gasping for breath.
              Having a bit of a crack with the lads, working a bit
              of overtime and complaining like mad at the shit
              conditions, the bastard foreman, the long hours
              and the shite pay, 'cos then I was happy.

CONNIE   Listen Albert, you can't decide when or where
              you're gonna die, but you can decide how you're
              gonna live.

              (*A long pause. He looks at her.*)

ALBERT   There's no point. Not without you.

CONNIE   Listen, a relationship doesn't end with death.

ALBERT   Well it doesn't exactly make it bloody blossom,
              does it?

CONNIE   We'll always be a team, you and me.

              (ALBERT *sits at the table, left.*)

ALBERT   Don't give me any of that 'I'll always be in the
              next room' rubbish, and 'talk to me like you always
              talked to me', 'cos it doesn't work.

CONNIE   Nobody can take away what happened between
              us. We'll always have that. That's between you
              and me and nobody else.

ALBERT   (*turning and looking at her*) Yes, but you're not
              here.

CONNIE   No, but you are, and I want you to make the most
              of what you've got. I want you to be happy.
              Albert, I want you to do it for me!

              (*Pause.* ALBERT *looks at her.*)

              Please. Do it for me.

              (*A long pause.* ALBERT *gets upset.*)

ALBERT   I can't Connie. I don't know how. Why couldn't it
          have been me? I wanted to go first. I never
          realised how much you meant to me until you
          weren't here any more and I had to cook me own
          meals an' that.

CONNIE   I'm touched.

ALBERT   I just want things to get back to normal.

CONNIE   What about Rose? She could be a big help.

ALBERT   That's cheered me up no end.

CONNIE   She could. You're just too stubborn. (*Pause –*
          CONNIE *hatches a plan.*) But you've upset her that
          many times she wouldn't help you now.

ALBERT   Good.

CONNIE   She can't stand you.

ALBERT   Give over, she bloody fancies me.

CONNIE   She thinks your pathetic.

ALBERT   She's dying to get her hands on me.

CONNIE   Yeah, to put em round your throat.

ALBERT   She bloody fancies me, it's obvious.

CONNIE   She said you were like a laxative.

ALBERT   What you talking about?

CONNIE   You irritate the shit out of her.

          (ALBERT *stands and moves away.*)

ALBERT   I'm ignoring you.

CONNIE   She feels sorry for you, always has done. She only
          humours you 'cos she's my friend. Where's all
          your friends? You haven't bloody got any.

ALBERT   I'd rather go out with Alice.

CONNIE	Would you?
ALICE	(*off*) Coooeee!
CONNIE	Well speak of the devil.
ALBERT	But –
CONNIE	Don't worry, she can't see or hear me.
ALICE	(*entering*) Albert, this is your lucky day!
ALBERT	Is it?

(ALICE *wears new, rather large teeth.*)

ALICE	Oh these, they're Joan's.
ALBERT	Who?
ALICE	From number twenty two. Well, they were her mam's, but she died.

(ALBERT *steps back in disgust.* CONNIE *sits at the table, left.*)

ALBERT	She bloody what?
ALICE	But these were her spare pair, silly. And Joan kept 'em. To remember her by! But she said I could borrow 'em. They're not the best fit but they'll do until mine arrive. What do you think?
ALBERT	I don't know what to bloody think any more.
ALICE	Do you like 'em?
ALBERT	(*sarcastically*) Bloody brilliant.
CONNIE	Well ask her then.
ALICE	But enough of me because today, it is your lucky day.
ALBERT	Is it?
ALICE	Because I have come to take you out.

ALBERT	What?
ALICE	To the Bingo.
ALBERT	Bingo!
ALICE	And we get a free kettle today.
ALBERT	Kettle!
CONNIE	It's what you make cups of tea with.
ALICE	You need to get out, you look terrible.
CONNIE	You look shocking.
ALICE	I'm a picture of health, 'cos I keep meself active. Cocky Night's been chasing me for years.
ALBERT	Well there's no danger there, 'cos Club Foot Cocky'll never catch you.
ALICE	I'm a bit of a man magnet.
ALBERT	Are ya?
ALICE	And since I've started wearing these teeth, I have to fight 'em off. Sex on legs, Cocky calls me.
ALBERT	I feel sick.
CONNIE	How can you resist that?
ALBERT	I'd love to, Alice –
ALICE	Well go on get your coat.
ALBERT	But . . . I'm already going out.
ALICE	But you've never been out for months.
CONNIE	You haven't.
ALBERT	I'm going out with . . . Rose. I promised Rose.
CONNIE	Well, well, well.
ALBERT	Shurrrup.

ALICE   What?

ALBERT   What!

ALICE   I thought you said something.

CONNIE   You did.

ALBERT   No.

ALICE   Well, you don't know what you're missing. 'Cos when I get me party head on, I'm like an animal. (*On her way past she gooses him.*) Easy, tiger.

(*She farts and exits, left.*)

ALBERT   Bloody hell, Alice!

(ALBERT *exits, right. A light on* CONNIE, *sat at the table.*)

CONNIE   And to keep Alice at arm's length, he arranged to take Rose to a dance. Bless him. The minute he'd arranged it he regretted it. He even went shopping for some new gear – but that was a bit of culture shock because Wrights Tower House had disappeared and when he went looking for C & A he ended up in Next where he actually bought some new clothes. The day of the dance arrived. He was eagerly looking forward to it.

(*Lights up on the room.* ALBERT *enters, wearing a posing pouch and carrying his clothes.*)

This is bloody obscene.

CONNIE   What the hell is that?

ALBERT   You said I had to get with the times.

CONNIE   I said you had to smarten yourself up not turn into Peter Stringfellow.

ALBERT   Does it make me bum look big?

CONNIE   It makes all of you look big.

ALBERT   Right, I'm taking it off.

CONNIE   Leave it. There isn't time, you'll be late.

ALBERT   I don't wanna go.

CONNIE   You'll enjoy it.

ALBERT   I bloody won't.

CONNIE   You won't with that attitude.

ALBERT   (*getting dressed*) What's the point in going then? This is your bloody fault, this.

CONNIE   It would be.

ALBERT   Nagging me. It's bloody uncomfortable.

CONNIE   Hurry up or you'll be late.

ALBERT   I'm not dancing.

CONNIE   It's a dance.

ALBERT   If she tries any funny business I'll –

CONNIE   Albert, have you heard yourself?

ALBERT   I'm not bloody bothered.

CONNIE   You look after her.

ALBERT   Would you like me to muzzle her or put her in a cage?

CONNIE   I'm warning you.

ALBERT   What if she throws herself at me?

CONNIE   You're only going to a dance.

ALBERT   What if she starts rubbing herself against me?

CONNIE   For God's sake.

ALBERT   What if –

CONNIE   What if! What if! What if you have a good time.
           That would be bloody unusual, wouldn't it? What
           if you have a good laugh?

ALBERT   I don't like laughing.

CONNIE   Albert, have you heard yourself!

ALBERT   Bloody women!

           (*Pause.*)

CONNIE   Albert.

ALBERT   What? (*He looks round.*) What is it?

CONNIE   You look –

ALBERT   What?

CONNIE   You look gorgeous.

ALBERT   Is it alright?

CONNIE   I'll say.

ALBERT   Are you sure? Right, here goes. (*He doesn't
           move.*) I'm away then. You sure I'm alright?

CONNIE   You'll be late.

ALBERT   Bloody hell!

           (ALBERT *goes to exit.* CONNIE *calls after him.*)

CONNIE   Albert!

           (ALBERT *checks.*)

           You look fantastic.

ALBERT   Bugger off.

           (ALBERT *exits.*)

CONNIE   (*to the audience*) No wonder I fell for him. I hope
           he enjoys himself. Mind, she can't dance like me,
           never could.

(Music in, 'Come Dance With Me'. CONNIE, in her own thoughts, dances round the room. Lights fade to spot on CONNIE and then out.)

Scene Two

Tea dance. ALBERT bursts in and starts to remove his smart clothes.

ROSE   *(off)* Alby! Alby!

            (She enters.)

            Alby!

ALBERT   It's fucking Albert!

ROSE   Well! I've never been . . . *(Slight pause.)* What have I done? *(Silence.)* You're gonna have to talk about it.

ALBERT   Just go.

ROSE   You can't go on like this.

ALBERT   Look, I can't do it. I can't put on a brave face and pretend everything's alright, 'cos it's not.

ROSE   It was only a dance.

CONNIE   You need to sort yourself out.

ALBERT   Bugger off. *(He realises who it is.)* Bloody hell!

ROSE   Don't you tell me to bugger off.

ALBERT   No, look, I just got scared.

CONNIE   Bless!

ALBERT   Don't start.

ROSE   Don't start what!

ALBERT   Don't start . . . going on at me.

ROSE	Why are you ignoring me?
ALBERT	I'm not.
CONNIE	You are.
ALBERT	(*to* CONNIE) I'm not.
ROSE	Calm down.
CONNIE	Yeah, calm down.
ALBERT	(*exasperated*) I am calm.
CONNIE	You're not.
ROSE	Then why are you shouting?
ALBERT	(*shouting*) I am not shouting!
CONNIE	Blood pressure.
ALBERT	Shurrup.
ROSE/ CONNIE	(*together*) Don't you talk to me like that.
ALBERT	I'm warning you.
ROSE	Warning me!
ALBERT	Rose . . .
ROSE	Who the hell do you think you are?
ALBERT	Rose . . .
CONNIE	You've done it now.
ROSE	Shouting your mouth off.
ALBERT	Look.
CONNIE	She's right.
ROSE	Ordering me about.
ALBERT	I didn't mean . . .

ROSE	Ungrateful.
CONNIE	You are.
ROSE	Bastard.
ALBERT	Rose . . .
ROSE	Don't touch me!
ALBERT	Listen . . .
ROSE	Don't talk to me.
ALBERT	(*shouting*) For God's sake will you just shut it for a minute!
	(*Silence.*)
CONNIE	He's so manly.
	(ALBERT *snaps a glare to her – she cowers.*)
ALBERT	I'm sorry, Rose. It's not you it's me. I can't come to terms with . . . well, with being without Connie.
CONNIE	Understandable, I suppose. (ALBERT *snaps a glare at her again.*) I'm a big miss.
ALBERT	I think you're a fantastic woman and you've been a great help and source of comfort to me, but I'm not ready to go dancing. I don't wanna enjoy meself.
CONNIE	You don't know how.
	(ALBERT *snaps another glare at her and she cowers again.*)
ALBERT	I'm grateful for everything you've done for me but, well, I need a bit of space to sort meself out. It's got nothing to do with you, it's me.
ROSE	I can help.
CONNIE	He's too bloody stubborn.
ROSE	Just answer me one question.

ALBERT   Yeah of course.

ROSE   Do you dislike me?

CONNIE   He dislikes everybody.

ALBERT   What?

ROSE   Do you hate me?

CONNIE   He doesn't even like himself.

ALBERT   No, no, of course I don't. I'm just finding things hard at the minute. It's not you, it's me. It's me, honest. Hell I've known you for years. You're probably . . . well the only friend I've got.

CONNIE   Friend?

ROSE   Well, do you fancy me?

ALBERT   What?

ROSE   I want to know.

CONNIE   So do I?

    (*Pause.*)

ALBERT   Well . . . you see . . . the thing is . . .

CONNIE   Yes . . .

ALBERT   I think you are a –

ROSE   Yes or no.

    (*Silence.*)

ALBERT   No.

ROSE   Nobody kisses me like that unless they really mean it.

CONNIE/   (*together*) Kisses you?
ALBERT

ROSE   Don't pretend you don't remember.

ALBERT   What are you talking about?

ROSE   That Christmas.

CONNIE   I'm gonna kill you.

ALBERT   That was four years ago.

ROSE/   So you remember then.
CONNIE

ALBERT   It meant nothing.

ROSE/   You remembered it though.
CONNIE

ALBERT   It was just a little kiss.

ROSE   That lasted five minutes.

ALBERT   You're exaggerating, she's exaggerating.

CONNIE   She's me best friend.

ROSE   You've fought it all these years.

CONNIE   I knew there was something funny going on that
            Christmas.

ALBERT   No.

CONNIE   Because you stopped wearing a vest and started
            driving faster.

ROSE   Look, I'll go.

            (ROSE *walks over to him and plants a smacker on
            his lips*.)

CONNIE   Well don't mind me.

ROSE   I knew you wouldn't forget.

            (*She exits.* ALBERT *profusely wipes it from his
            lips*.)

CONNIE   A little kiss!

ALBERT   (*buying time*) What?

CONNIE   A little kiss.

ALBERT   I thought I wasn't allowed to touch you.

CONNIE   You know what I mean.

ALBERT   It meant nothing.

CONNIE   *Liar.*

ALBERT   You know what she's like.

CONNIE   Yes I bloody do.

ALBERT   She was teasing me, like she always does, so I
              called her bluff, that was all. I thought bugger it.
              So I kissed her, full on the lips and just as I
              thought, she shit herself and ran a bloody mile. It
              was a way of getting rid of her.

CONNIE   You like her though, don't you?

ALBERT   No.

CONNIE   You enjoyed it.

ALBERT   I didn't.

CONNIE   I'm not stupid.

ALBERT   Have you changed?

              (ALBERT *moves to the table, left, and sits.* CONNIE
              follows and stands, confronting him.)

CONNIE   I want you to like her. And you do, but you're
              just too stubborn to admit it. Listen to me for once
              in your life, you musn't feel guilty about moving
              on.

ALBERT   I don't want to move on. You see, I miss ya'. It's
              not the big things that are important it's the little
              things. The way you used to contradict everything
              I said.

CONNIE   I did not.

           (ALBERT *gives her a knowing look.*)

ALBERT   I even miss you farting in bed and that used to
           make me feel sick.

CONNIE   Can you get it through that thick skull of yours
           that I don't mind. You musn't feel lonely.

ALBERT   How the hell can I feel lonely when you're
           nagging at me every two bloody minutes?

CONNIE   But I won't be here forever. I can't be here
           forever. When your dead they write on your
           gravestone when you were born and when you
           died, but what matters is the hyphen in the middle.

ALBERT   I'm ignoring you.

           (*He goes and sits in the armchair.*)

CONNIE   Albert, I want you to get rid of my clothes.

ALBERT   What?

CONNIE   They're holding you back. You have to burn them,
           sell them, anything –

ALBERT   No. Never. I can't. Don't ask me. I'm not.

CONNIE   You have to. I'm not asking you to forget about
           me Albert, I'm asking you to start living a bit.
           Bloody hell Albert, you used to be so alive, so full
           of big ideas. You were the life and soul of any
           party with your jokes and your quick wit. You
           turned my head. But now look at you.

           (*He looks himself up and down.*)

           When was the last time you did something
           impulsive? Bought something you didn't need.
           Did something you shouldn't. Where's the man I
           married? I'm wasting my time. Unless you do
           something to move on I'm not coming back.

           (*She exits.*)

ALBERT   Connie! I'm sorry.

                (*He looks round and comes to realise that she has
                left him.*)

                Connie! Connie! Lets talk about it. Bloody hell,
                Connie! Come back. This isn't funny. I'm gonna
                count to three. One . . . two . . . Connie. I'll put
                some Frank on, we'll have a dance. Right, I'm
                putting it on.

                (*Music: Frank Sinatra, 'You Make Me Feel So
                Young'.*)

                Now I'm starting to dance.

                (ALICE *enters. She stands watching him.*)

                Come on. Come on. Dance with me.

ALICE   She's dead, Albert. You have to let go.

ALBERT   Look Alice, I don't mean to be rude but I can do
                without this now.

                (ALBERT *sits at the table.*)

ALICE   I am not staying.

                (*She sits.*)

ALBERT   Good.

ALICE   I am the bringer of bad news.

ALBERT   Don't tell me you've got a sister.

ALICE   You won't be seeing me for awhile.

ALBERT   That is devastating.

                (*He moves right and hangs his jacket up on the
                hook.*)

ALICE   I'm sorry but I'm going away on holiday, with
                Cocky. He's asked me to marry him.

ALBERT   Alice?

ALICE   He won't take no for an answer. Cocky by name, Cocky by nature.

ALBERT   (*sitting in his armchair*) Alice!

ALICE   We were in Tesco and I didn't see him coming and he caught me by the cabbages. Me Brussels were all over the floor, but I managed to hang on to me Victoria Sponge and coconut macaroons. And then he just popped it out.

ALBERT   He would do.

ALICE   (*dragging her chair over to* ALBERT) 'I want you to be the woman I spend the rest of my life with', he said. I didn't know where to put meself. But I'm not easy, I said, a woman needs time to think these things through, but he was like one of them gigolo's. And then, in true Toreador tradition two tickets to Torremolinos were thrust into my hand. And that's not easy to say with these teeth, I can tell you. So we're going to Spain on Saturday so he can persuade me to marry him. I think he wants sex. (*Pause.*) Albert, I think he wants sex.

ALBERT   Well that's the problem with marriage, they come to expect it.

ALICE   You know . . . on average, how many times a week did you, ya know, do it?

ALBERT   Alice . . .

ALICE   I need to know.

ALBERT   Well . . . it's like this, on a good week, you can get away without doing it at all.

ALICE   We'll see about that. Anyway I can't stay and chat to you all day, I've got an appointment at Tanfastic.

     (ALICE *exits. Instrumental of 'All the Way' plays.* ALBERT *tidies up the room and fetches an empty cardboard box from the kitchen and places it on the table as the lights slowly fade.*)

Scene Three

Lights up as ALBERT *opens the wardrobe door. Music fades out. He carefully takes out* CONNIE'S *coat. He holds it, smells and with great difficulty he very carefully folds it and as he places it in the box, music comes in: Frank Sinatra, 'They Can't Take That Away From Me'.*

During the song, with great difficulty he empties the contents of the wardrobe into the box and takes it out. On returning, he goes to shut the wardrobe doors and notices a photograph on the floor. He picks it up and looks at it, stunned.

Lights fade to black.

Scene Four

Lights up. ROSE *appears in the doorway.*

ALBERT   Thanks for coming.

             (*Silence.*)

             Would you like to sit down? (*No reaction.*) Can I get you a drink or anything? Would you like a Snowball?

             (*They exchange looks.*)

ROSE   Gin and Tonic.

ALBERT   Right. Good. (*He pours her drink.*) It's a lot of weather we've been having lately. Your hair looks nice. (*Handing her the drink.*) Look, thanks for coming.

ROSE   You said that.

ALBERT   Did I? Well I mean it. Look, I know I haven't been ... well I know I have been a bit of a miserable old get, but I just want you to know that it's nothing personal. You have to laugh, haven't you?

(*She glares at him.*)

I mean I think your . . . I really like . . . I've been thinking, you and Connie were good friends for a long time and . . . you know . . . she would want you and me to continue to be friends so I thought that perhaps we could go out for dinner. That is if you want to. I mean, if you don't want to I would understand, but I thought that it would be nice if you would want to. Would you like to go out to dinner?

(ROSE *looks at him.*)

We could go anywhere. You pick.

ROSE   The Tontine.

ALBERT   It's bloody expens . . . yeah, the Tontine. Right.

(ROSE *starts to exit.*)

I love the Tontine. Yeah, the Tontine's brilliant. It's got a lovely ambience.

(*Slight pause.*)

I've got rid of Connie's clothes. All of 'em. They're gone.

ROSE   Oh, Albert!

ALBERT   And I found this.

(*He shows her the photograph.*)

ROSE   Oh!

ALBERT   Who is he, Rose? (*Silence.*) I need to know. Rose, I need to know.

(ROSE *takes a deep breath.*)

ROSE   He's a dance partner, that's all. They used to dance together.

ALBERT   Dance partner?

ROSE   You see, when we went dancing, she wasn't my
            partner she was his.

ALBERT   What was his name?

ROSE   Does it matter?

ALBERT   (*shouting*) It does to me!

ROSE   Arthur. His name's Arthur. Arthur Winstanley.

ALBERT   Right.

ROSE   Connie wanted you to go. She begged you to go
            but you wouldn't.

ALBERT   I had to work.

ROSE   You always had to work. Your problems is that
            you didn't work to live, you lived to work.

ALBERT   You have to have money.

ROSE   And where did Connie fit in?

ALBERT   I was doing it for her.

ROSE   Were you? Were you really doing it for her?

ALBERT   I can't believe she didn't tell me?

ROSE   And what would you have said? 'That's okay
            darling, you go and enjoy yourself'.

ALBERT   I just didn't think she could be that deceitful. I
            didn't think we had any secrets.

ROSE   Wake up. Every couple has secrets. They'd never
            survive otherwise.

ALBERT   Oh God! Listen, did she . . . I mean did they . . .
            you know, were they . . .

ROSE   And would it make a difference if they were?

ALBERT   'Course it would make a bloody difference.

ROSE   No! No they weren't.

ALBERT   You're just saying that.

ROSE   Then you don't know Connie. Heaven knows why,
              but she was devoted to you.

ALBERT   It bloody looks like it.

ROSE   I'm not gonna pretend that she didn't enjoy it,
              because she did. She used to have a good laugh.

ALBERT   I can have a good laugh. I'm bloody great at
              laughing.

ROSE   But the truth is he liked her a bit more and one
              night he got a bit carried away and he came on to
              her.

ALBERT   He what!

ROSE   But she wouldn't entertain it. She stopped going,
              just like that. Maybe she was afraid of her own
              feelings, I dunno. She liked him, but she loved the
              dancing and the freedom, the getting out of the
              house for awhile. And when it stopped, by hell
              she missed it. But she didn't want to hurt you.
              You see Albert, you were her first, her last and her
              only. You didn't know what you had. And the
              funny thing is Albert, not many people do – until
              it is too late.

ALBERT   But I loved her.

ROSE   That's as may be, but people appreciate being
              appreciated, and you just took her for granted.

ALBERT   Oh, God.

ROSE   She loved you.

ALBERT   I wanna make it up to her. I wanna do it different. I
              wanna start again. What can I do about it now?

ROSE   Well you can stop feeling sorry for yourself for a
              start. Do you think she would want to see you like
              this? You only retired from work, not from living.
              I've still got a bush that needs some attention.

(ALBERT *smiles*.)

But if the offer is still on, you can start by taking me to the Tontine. Come on.

(*Pause*)

ALBERT   I can't.

(ROSE *goes and gets* ALBERT'S *coat*.)

ROSE   Come on, Albert. Or do you want me to tell people you got me here under false pretences?

(*He turns and looks at her*.)

Come on, let's flash the cash. Oway.

(*Music: Frank Sinatra, 'I Get a Kick Out of You'. CONNIE enters and stands in a pool of light, right*.)

CONNIE   And they did. Albert felt uncomfortable and confused, like he usually did when he wasn't in control of the situation. He didn't really want to be there but he didn't have any options. He was nervous. Rose went to the toilet and Albert stood there, feeling conspicuous as though everyone in the place was looking at him.

(*She moves up right and watches the next scene*.)

Scene Five

Lights up on the table, left. ALBERT *sits holding a menu. He lowers the menu and peers over the top of it. He looks round the room. Noticing the prices, he lowrs the menu and mouths, 'fucking hell'.*

Music out. He starts to whistle, 'There maybe trouble ahead', from 'Let's Face the Music and Dance'. ROSE *returns from the toilet. She waits to be seated and looks at the chair.* ALBERT *wants to know what she is looking at and also looks at the chair. She nods towards the chair.* ALBERT *looks at it again. Disgusted, she pulls the chair out and sits.*

ALBERT   (*attempting to be humorous*) Everything come out alright?

(ROSE *is unamused. Silence. They look round.*)

A lot of weather we've been having lately.

(*Pause.*)

ALBERT   You know why the Australians call it Four-X, 'cos they can't spell piss.

(*Silence.* ROSE *is not amused.* ALBERT *is slightly embarrassed.*)

ROSE   I'm hungry.

ALBERT   You would be.

ROSE   What?

ALBERT   Look Rose, I don't think I can do this.

ROSE   And why not? What you gonna do? Go home and stare into the fire?

ALBERT   I just keep seeing him and her.

ROSE   I'm gonna punch you in a minute. She was many things, but she wasn't unfaithful.

ALBERT   Do you know something. I know. I know that, but I still –

ROSE   Well, bugger it then. Come on, I think I'll have the lobster.

(ALBERT *pauses a second and then looks at her before checking the menu for the price.*)

ALBERT   You would do. Reasonable, an' all. I'll have to remortgage the bloody house.

ROSE   Listen, if it'll help I'll go halves.

ALBERT   Halves. You will not go halves. I won't allow it.
            You can pay for the lot. I mean, who's grieving
            here?

ROSE   You tight bugger.

ALBERT   I'm only kidding, you keep your money. I can
            spend me life's savings on one bloody meal.

ROSE   Hey, who's that over there?

ALBERT   Where?

ROSE   It's thingy.

ALBERT   Who?

ROSE   Off the telly.

ALBERT   So it is.

ROSE   He bloody loves himself.

ALBERT   Look at 'em all watching him.

ROSE   They're pathetic.

ALBERT   (*shouting*) Let him get on with his meal.

ROSE   Albert.

ALBERT   Well, poor bugger.

ROSE   It's embarrassing.

ALBERT   Why can't they all just leave him alone?

ROSE   He's just human.

ALBERT   Look at 'em all staring.

ROSE   I can't look. It's embarrassing. I can't look. I just
            can't look.

ALBERT   Force yourself.

ROSE   No, I can't look, it's disgusting.

(*She looks away.*)

ALBERT   He's having salmon.

                (*She snaps back.*)

ROSE   Is he? I was gonna have the salmon.

ALBERT   Probably didn't cost enough.

ROSE   I like salmon.

ALBERT   Who's he with?

ROSE   I dunno, but she looks a right sight.

ALBERT   (*likes her*) Oh, I dunno.

ROSE   Oh, come on. Would you wear a dress like that?

ALBERT   Well, not personally, no.

ROSE   Oh look, he's coming this way.

                (*They both sit up and smile rather falsely as the
                imaginary celebrity walks past. He ignores them.
                They're disappointed.*)

ALBERT   He looks thinner.

ROSE   Yeah, on top.

ALBERT   Connie used to like him.

ROSE   Yeah, but her taste in men left a lot to be desired.

ALBERT   Do you think? (*Beat.*) Funny!

ROSE   Connie would have had –

ROSE/   (*together*) . . . the pancakes.
ALBERT

ALBERT   It didn't matter, savoury or sweet.

ROSE   She used to love flippin' 'em over, didn't she?
                She was a master at it.

ALBERT   I'll say. Mine used to end up stuck to the ceiling or on the floor.

ROSE   You always were a useless tosser.

> (*They both laugh. Music: Frank Sinatra, 'You're Getting To Be a Habit With Me'.* CONNIE *moves down into her light.*)

CONNIE   And they spent most of the night talking about me. Sharing stories and tales that the other didn't know. And Albert laughed. I know it's hard to believe, but he did. He enjoyed himself. I could tell he enjoyed himself, 'cos he give the waiter a tip. It's the first time I'd ever known him tip anybody while he was sober. Rose and Albert started to see a bit of each other. Albert sorted out her bush and she sorted out his washing. They were company for each other. I just kept out of the way and let them get on with it.

> (*She exits.*)

Scene Six

Lights rise. Music fades out. ROSE *is sitting at the table doing a puzzle from a woman's magazine.* ALBERT *is in his armchair, reading the Daily Mirror.*

ALBERT   They're not very chewy, these toffees.

ROSE   They're hard.

ALBERT   I like chewy toffees.

ROSE   I'll not go there again.

ALBERT   Thorntons?

ROSE   No, these aren't Thorntons!

ALBERT   I thought –

ROSE   These are too hard.

ALBERT   Thorntons are creamier.

ROSE   And more chewy. I got these off the market.

ALBERT   You can tell.

ROSE   I feel a bit chilly.

ALBERT   Well, put a bloody cardigan on.

ROSE   You never put the fire on.

ALBERT   'Cos it's not cold.

ROSE   I'm freezin'.

ALBERT   The fire goes on in the winter.

ROSE   It's January.

ALBERT   I'm alright.

ROSE   There's a good film on at the cinemas. *Road to Perdition*.

ALBERT   The Road films. Bob Hope and Dorothy Lamour?

ROSE   I don't know.

ALBERT   He's dead, isn't he?

ROSE   Yeah. Toffee?

ALBERT   They're too hard. I would you give you a sugared almond.

ROSE   Me favourite!

ALBERT   But I haven't got any . . .

          (*Pause.* ALBERT *goes to the table and stands close to* ROSE.)

          You do know that, Connie's the only person for me?

ROSE   Where did that come from?

ALBERT   No one will ever take her place.

ROSE   Nobody's trying to.

ALBERT   We were soul mates.

ROSE   I know.

ALBERT   She had a personality.

ROSE   What are you trying to say?

ALBERT   She was special.

ROSE   I only offered you a toffee.

            (ALBERT *walks to the armchair, picks up his
            paper and throws it back on the chair. A pause.*)

ALBERT   I've bought you a ticket.

ROSE   For the pictures.

ALBERT   No, I thought we could go on holiday.

ROSE   A holiday!

ALBERT   Me and you.

ROSE   Bloody hell.

ALBERT   I mean if you don't want to –

ROSE   It's just a bit sudden, that's all.

ALBERT   I thought we might go to New Zealand.

ROSE   New Zealand!

ALBERT   Yeah.

ROSE   New Zealand!

ALBERT   To see our Judith.

ROSE   It's a long way.

ALBERT   Yeah.

ROSE   It's the other side of the world.

ALBERT   I don't need a bloody geography lesson.

ROSE   I don't know what to say.

ALBERT   (*moving quickly to* ROSE) We stop off in
          Singapore and then we go on to New Zealand.
          We're staying at our Judith's. I thought we could
          go out there for six weeks.

ROSE   Six weeks!

ALBERT   It's the other side of the world.

ROSE   I don't know what to say.

ALBERT   I wasn't keen on going on me own so I've bought
          you a ticket. You don't have to pay me back or
          'owt.

ROSE   But . . . but New Zealand?

          (*Pause.*)

ALBERT   Well, are you coming or not?

ROSE   We'd have to pack a lot of sandwiches.

ALBERT   So you're coming then?

          (*She stands and moves down centre, away from
          him.*)

ROSE   Well, I don't know. I'll need time to think.

ALBERT   What do you need time to think for?

ROSE   It's a long way.

ALBERT   I know.

ROSE   It's the other side of the world.

          (*He moves down to join her.*)

ALBERT   Look, I think we've established where it is. Are
          you coming or not?

(*Pause.* ROSE *releases a smile.*)

ROSE   Yeah. Alright then.

ALBERT   You'll come?

ROSE   I'd love to come.

ALBERT   With me?

ROSE   It would be an honour.

ALBERT   Right.

ROSE   I feel funny.

ALBERT   We're going next month.

ROSE   Next month! We're going next month? That's not
            enough time to get ready. It's the other side of
            the world.

ALBERT   I bloody know where it is.

ROSE   Don't you think that's a bit impulsive?

ALBERT   Yeah.

ROSE   A bloody month. Bloody hell, I'll have loads to
            sort out. I'll have to go and sort out. (*She pauses
            and stares at* ALBERT.) You're a dark horse, Albert
            Nobbs.

            (*She moves towards him and kisses him. He
            receives it. As they kiss,* CONNIE *enters. As* ROSE
            and ALBERT *part,* CONNIE *is staring at* ALBERT.)

ROSE   Thanks Albert. I'll see you later.

            (ROSE *exits.* CONNIE *and* ALBERT *stare at each
            other.*)

ALBERT   Is that what you wanted?

CONNIE   I want you to be happy.

ALBERT   Is that what you wanted?

CONNIE   Is it what you want?

           (*Pause.*)

           Have you done this just for me?

ALBERT   No.

CONNIE   I don't want you to do it just for me.

ALBERT   The other night I woke up 'cos I heard you
           shouting. And then I got up and I went looking
           round the house to try and find you. And I wasn't
           sure whether I was awake or asleep. But I expected
           to see you. I was convinced that I'd see you. And
           you weren't there. The house was so quiet. I
           didn't know quietness could be that empty. And I
           made up my mind there and then, if I can't have
           you, then I'm going to be with your . . . our
           daughter . . . and our granddaughter. 'Cos they're
           ours, they've come from you and me. And they're
           alive.

CONNIE   You'll have to fly.

ALBERT   I thought we might walk.

CONNIE   In an aeroplane.

ALBERT   Bloody stop it.

CONNIE   What about your cholestrol and your Warfarin?

ALBERT   You only live once, Connie.

           (CONNIE *smiles.*)

CONNIE   You always were impulsive.

ALBERT   Rash, that's me.

CONNIE   Tell me about it.

           (*Pause.*)

ALBERT   I want to be able to hold you.

CONNIE   (*sensitively*) No, Albert.

ALBERT   Just for a minute.

CONNIE   We can't.

ALBERT   You always had a beautiful body.

CONNIE   I wish.

ALBERT   Nobody did things to me like you did. Even with all those wrinkles, you looked good.

CONNIE   Charming!

ALBERT   I'd give anything to see your body for one last time.

CONNIE   Albert!

ALBERT   Please!

CONNIE   Albert.

ALBERT   Just one last time.

CONNIE   I can't.

ALBERT   'Course you can. For me. Do it for me.

           (*A long pause. Music: Frank Sinatra, 'Anything Goes'. Slowly* CONNIE *starts to undo her top. Lights fade to black.*)

Scene Seven

ROSE *paces the floor.* ALBERT *enters, his trousers soaking wet.*

ROSE   Where the hell have you been?

ALBERT   Out.

ROSE   Look at the state of your trousers! You're bloody soaking.

ALBERT   I went for a walk.

ROSE	A walk!
ALBERT	Up Tinker's Alley.
ROSE	Tinker's bloody Alley. It's six in the morning.
ALBERT	And I saw this Tarzan swing.
ROSE	I don't believe this.
ALBERT	So I went on it.
ROSE	. . . Albert.
ALBERT	And I fell in.
ROSE	I don't know what the hell is going on but you had better get changed out of those wet things before you catch your death, and hurry up.
ALBERT	(*as he exits*) And I'm gonna start playing football again.
ROSE	We have a plane to catch and you're out playing silly buggers. Is it me? Are you doing this just to have a go at me? Is it because you're afraid of flying, is that it? Are you trying to put things off?
ALBERT	(*off*) No.
ROSE	Well I don't understand it. I don't know what's got into you lately. Playing on a bloody Tarzan at your age. You ought to have more sense. Are you packed?
ALBERT	(*off*) Yes.
ROSE	Have you got your passport?
ALBERT	(*off*) Yes!
ROSE	You're a bloody liablity. I've been worried sick.

(ALBERT *appears, dressed in a football kit that is far too small. He carries another shirt and a pair of shoes that he places on the armchair.*)

ROSE   Oh my God!

ALBERT   I found it at the back of the cupboard.

ROSE   You're doing this on purpose!

ALBERT   Still fits.

ROSE   Just to have a go.

ALBERT   And I've bought some new boots.

ROSE   Albert!

ALBERT   They're in the case.

ROSE   I don't know what's going on, but I can't stand it. Right, I'm gonna wait in the car, heaven help you if we miss that plane.

(ROSE *exits*. CONNIE *appears*.)

CONNIE   You daft old bugger!

ALBERT   Hey, I could play a bit, couldn't I, Con?

CONNIE   Better than Wilfy Mannion, Albert.

ALBERT   I wish.

(ALBERT *goes to the hall and returns dragging a suitcase and carrying a huge carton of sandwiches*.)

Hey, I'm gonna start playing again – for the Boy's Club.

CONNIE   The Boys Club!

ALBERT   Over thiry-fives.

CONNIE   But you're over sixty.

ALBERT   Case weighs a bloody ton . . .

CONNIE   Oh you haven't. Tell me you haven't.

ALBERT   I don't like spicy food.

CONNIE   Oh Albert, for God's sake, you're going to New Zealand. And you'll never get it all through customs.

              (*Noticing the carton of sandwiches.*)

              What's that?

ALBERT   Sandwiches.

CONNIE   They feed you on the plane.

ALBERT   It's a long flight.

CONNIE   How many have you got this time?

ALBERT   Twenty-seven. Hey, we don't go over Iraq, do we?

CONNIE   No!

ALBERT   Thank God for that. I shouldn't have done this. What was I thinking about?

CONNIE   Stop panicking and go and get ready. NOW!

              (ALBERT *changes shirts and puts on his shoes.*)

              You're like a big bloody kid.

ALBERT   (*off*) Here we go.

CONNIE   You've got the IQ of a rubber duck.

ALBERT   (*off*) Funny!

CONNIE   You're a bloody big baby, you always have been. Anything to do with heights and you're gone.

ALBERT   (*off*) Oh, we're on to this again, are we?

CONNIE   You started panicking on Debenham's escalator.

ALBERT   (*off*) Have you finished!

CONNIE   In fact, you're not so clever going upstairs.

ALBERT   (*off*) Connie!

CONNIE   So calm down, everything'll be fine.

            (ALBERT *enters, dressing.*)

ALBERT   Fine! I've had three shits this morning. And it's
            only half past six.

CONNIE   How about a dance then, Fred?

ALBERT   On a bloody Monday morning?

CONNIE   Yeah.

            (*Pause.* ALBERT *looks at her. She smiles.*)

ALBERT   Yeah, why not? Bugger it. If you wanna dance you
            can have a dance, you can have anything you
            want – but I thought that I couldn't touch . . .

CONNIE   Bugger it.

ALBERT   (*moving to the CDs, up centre*) What would you
            like on? (*He turns and faces her, speaking with
            affection.*) A bit of Barry?

CONNIE   A bit of Frank?

            (ALBERT *smiles.*)

ALBERT   Frank! Fantastic. Now you're talking. I knew
            you'd come round to my way of thinking. He's
            great, isn't he? It's his phrasing.

            (*He puts on a CD – Frank Sinatra, 'I'm Gonna
            Live Until I Die'. Very slowly they come together.
            As they touch,* ALBERT *melts and relishes the
            moment.* CONNIE *smiles at him. He returns the
            compliment. They dance happily until* ALBERT'S
            *back gives way. He emits a groan and then moves
            upstage to switch off the CD.*)

ALBERT   We're not as young as we used to be, Con.

CONNIE   No, Albert. Albert, I'm going now.

ALBERT   What?

CONNIE   Time's up. You don't need me any more.

ALBERT   What you talking about? 'Course I need you. No, please. It's the trip, isn't it? I'll cancel it. Is it Rose? I won't see her –

CONNIE   No, it's not that.

ALBERT   You have to stay –

CONNIE   Don't.

ALBERT   I can't live without –

CONNIE   Albert, stop it.

ALBERT   But –

CONNIE   Stop it. You're doing very canny. You'll be alright.

ALBERT   I won't. I'm useless. You know I am. I can't shit properly unless you're there.

CONNIE   STOP IT. Stop it. Please don't make this difficult for me.

ALBERT   I'll never love –

CONNIE   Don't. There's no need to say it. There's no need to say anything. Albert, come here.

          (*They move together and prepare to kiss. At the decisive moment*, ROSE *enters.*)

ROSE   Bloody hell, Albert!

ALBERT   Every bloody time!

          (CONNIE *moves away.*)

ROSE   What are you stood like that for?

ALBERT   Like what?

ROSE   Like you're constipated.

ALBERT   Rose, for God's sake!

ROSE	Well are you ready yet?
ALBERT	Rose, will you just give me a minute, for God's sake.
ROSE	I'm in the car. Hurry up or we'll miss the plane.
ALBERT	Bugger off.
CONNIE	You're getting on better then.
	(ROSE *exits. Music in, an instrumental version of 'All the Way'.*)
CONNIE	You take care of her.
ALBERT	She'll have to buck her bloody ideas up a bit.
CONNIE	Right, Albert.
ALBERT	You always did things to me, Connie.
CONNIE	(*pause*) Say hello to our Judith for me.
ALBERT	She's a lovely kid!
CONNIE	Like her mother.
ALBERT	No, she's nice.
CONNIE	And don't let Mandy forget me.
ALBERT	Forget ya! No bloody chance. Me case is full of photographs.
CONNIE	Our Mandy. Enjoy her, Albert! Treasure her.
ALBERT	Don't worry about that.
CONNIE	And give her a big cuddle from her old grandma.
ALBERT	I'm gonna squeeze her bloody head off.
CONNIE	You will, an' all.
ALBERT	You'd better believe it.
	(*He is overcome.*)

CONNIE   You have a good time.

ALBERT   (*through the tears*) Don't worry, do you know
            how much it's bloody cost.

CONNIE   Albert Nobbs!

            (ALBERT, *crying, stares at her. She moves towards
            the exit.*)

            Don't you go soft on me or I'll knock your bloody
            head off. (*He is overcome, but fights it.*) If you
            had the chance, would you do it all again?

ALBERT   And some.

CONNIE   And me. We had some arguments, didn't we . . .

ALBERT   And I loved every one of them.

            (CONNIE *turns to exit and checks.*)

CONNIE   Hey –

ALBERT   What?

CONNIE   Don't forget to put the bin out.

            (ROSE *enters from USL, shouting.*)

ROSE   Albert! Bloody hell, Albert. What the hell is
            going on?

            (ALBERT *turns to deal with* ROSE.)

ALBERT   Rose! Will you just give me a minute?

            (ROSE *exits. He turns back to face* CONNIE. *She is
            gone.*)

ALBERT   (*sitting*) Oh my God!

            (ALBERT *is lost.* ROSE *sticks her head back in.*)

ROSE   Albert, we're gonna miss the plane.

            (*She re-enters, sensing that something is not
            right. Her tone is soft and caring. A long pause.*)

ROSE   You alright, Albert? (*Pause.*) It'll be alright. (*Pause.*) It's a big aeroplane and they fly every day.

(ALBERT *glares at her.*)

Shall I wait in the car?

ALBERT   No. Stay.

(*A CD jumps out of the case and crashes on to the floor. They both look at it.*)

ROSE   Bloody hell, I shit meself. (*She picks it up.*) Barry Manilow.

(ALBERT *looks up.*)

ALBERT   I've been looking for that.

(*He takes the CD.*)

ROSE   I thought you hated Barry Manilow.

ALBERT   Who told you that?

ROSE   You did.

ALBERT   You don't listen, that's your trouble. I bloody love Barry Manilow.

ROSE   But you said –

ALBERT   He's one of my favourites.

ROSE   We're gonna have to get going?

(*He pauses for a moment then he puts his coat on.*)

ALBERT   I'm sitting next to the window on the plane, so you can bugger off.

ROSE   You promised me.

ALBERT   I paid for the tickets. Get me case.

ROSE   Charming.

(ROSE *struggles with the case.*)

What the hell have you got in here, a dead body?

ALBERT Hurry up or we'll miss the plane.

(ROSE *gives him a filthy look as she drags the case off.* ALBERT *has one last look round the room.*)

Have I taken me tablets? Did you see me take me tablets?

(*Music plays, Frank Sinatra's 'That's Life'. He notices the plant on the unit and places it in the very centre of the table. He spots the Barry Manilow CD on the arm of the chair, picks it up, studies it, smiles and then exits.*)